SHAKESPE[...]

AND THE

FOUNDERS OF LIBERTY IN AMERICA

BY

CHARLES MILLS GAYLEY, Litt.D., LL.D.

PROFESSOR OF THE ENGLISH LANGUAGE AND LITERATURE IN THE
UNIVERSITY OF CALIFORNIA

New York
THE MACMILLAN COMPANY
1917

PREFACE

In this period of conflict, the sternest that the world has known, when we have joined heart and hand with Great Britain, it may profit Americans to recall how essentially at one with Englishmen we have always been in everything that counts. That the speech, the poetry, of the race are ours and theirs in common, we know—they are Shakespeare. But that the institutions, the law and the liberty, the democracy administered by the fittest, are not only theirs and ours in common, but are derived from Shakespeare's England, and are Shakespeare, too, we do not generally know or, if we have known, we do not always remember.

"Shakespeare and the Founders of Liberty in America!" exclaims the genial humorist. "What does the man mean?—That Shakespeare hobnobbed with Washington or helped Jefferson write the Declaration of Independence?" Hardly; but something not itself altogether lacking in the element of surprise: that Shakespeare was acquainted with more than one of the English statesmen who wrested from King James the colonial charters by which, between 1606 and 1620, English liberty was first planted in Virginia and New England—individual freedom and equality, due process of the law and independence of the courts, trial by jury, the right of representative assembly, and government by consent of the governed; that Shakespeare had confidential relations with these English patriots, the founders of American liberty, and that these relations are proved by the contents and source of one of his plays; that Shakespeare was in sympathy with the teachings of the moral and political master of the liberal movement, and that this sympathy is manifest in many of the poet's works.

The purpose of this book is to show, moreover, that the thoughts and even the words of the liberal master, the judicious Hooker, passed into the minds of our Revolutionary Fathers and into the Declaration of Independence; and that the principles common to Shakespeare and Hooker, to Sir Edwin Sandys, Southampton, and the other Patriots of seventeenth-century England, several of them Shakespeare's friends, are the principles of liberty which America enjoys today. The purpose is, also, to remind Americans that the eleven-hundred-year heritage of language and literature, of race, of custom, of law, of spirit energizing toward freedom—civil and religious—of political development, cherished by Britons at home and Britons in the American colonies in Shakespeare's time, did not cease with the American Revolution; that the colonists were but asserting their rights as Englishmen under charter and common law, and that the hearts of the truest and noblest Englishmen at home were with them in the struggle; that the heritage of today is a heritage which for fourteen hundred years has been ripening for the British Empire and America alike.

The political part of this heritage is the common property of the triad of great modern democracies—in order of birth, the United States of America, the union of free commonwealths styled the British Empire, the present French Republic. But the nursing mother of all three was the liberal England of Shakespeare and Hooker and their friends among the Patriots of early seventeenth-century England. What wonder that in the agony of the twentieth century these sister democracies march side by side that military autocracy may perish from the face of the earth!

To the descendants of Virginia Britannia and the Mayflower and of the American Revolution, to the descendants of their English brothers—the Patriots of Stuart England and the Britain of George III, and to the descendants of Lafayette and Beaumarchais and Rochambeau,—to the descendants not of the blood alone but of the spirit, of the heart and conscience, the faith and stern resolve, the undying devotion to freedom, right, and unconquerable hope, this little book is dedicated.

CHARLES MILLS GAYLEY.

BERKELEY, CALIFORNIA,
November 3, 1917.

CONTENTS

Shakespeare and the Founders of Liberty in America

CHAPTER I

THE FOUNDATIONS OF LIBERTY IN AMERICA

THE incomparable seamen and adventurers who in Elizabeth's reign swept Spain from the seas, and bridled the West Indies and the Northern continents for English enterprise, colonization, law and speech,— Drake and Frobisher, Davis, Hawkins, Gilbert and Raleigh—were compatriots of our forefathers and pioneers of our American history. Those were the years of Shakespeare's youth: when he whipped his top in the school-yard behind the Guild Hall of Stratford; when he walked each night the hawthorn lane to Shottery; when he bade farewell to Henley Street; when he played his first parts with Leicester's company in London. The adventurers and planters of Virginia, in later years when Shakespeare was writing Troilus and Cressida, Coriolanus, and The Tempest, were of his blood and temper, the blood and temper of the forefathers of many of us today. Their ventures and failures, their faults and virtues, are our history, Anglo-Saxon and American, as well as theirs.

It was a group of patriots clustered about Shakespeare's patron, the Earl of Southampton, and Sir Edwin Sandys, Southampton's ally—a group of patriots, some of them friends of Shakespeare, some of them acquaintances,—that laid the foundations of constitutional government in the New World.

They were the leaders of the Liberal, or Independent party in the Virginia Company of London, several of them leaders of that party in Parliament, too. Looking at first for redress from James I of abuses which toward the end of Elizabeth's reign had run to a somewhat perilous excess—favoritism, monopoly, subsidy, interference with control of taxation, with freedom of election, person and speech, and with other political inheritance of the Commons—they soon found that under the new régime they had leaped from the frying pan into the fire. In the charter of 1606, granted for the establishment of plantations in Virginia, the future inhabitants and their posterity were to have "all liberties, franchises, and immunities" of British subjects; but the King had "reserved to himself the right to furnish the form of government for the companies in England and plantations in America, and also to appoint the officials to execute the same. . . . The plantations and companies were directly under the political control of the Crown. . . . The members of the council in America had the right of suffrage among themselves; but they were representatives of an absolute king. The planters had no control over them, and little

or no part in the government, which was imperial."
The people had no political power. The industrial
system was to be balefully communistic, that of "a
vast stock farm, or collection of farms, worked by
servants who were to receive, in return for their
labor, all their necessaries and a share in the proceeds
of the undertaking." [1]

From 1608 on, the Patriots, as they were called, of
the company in London set their faces toward
reform—none more zealously than the Earl of
Southampton and Sir Edwin Sandys. The former
had long been interested in schemes for colonization.
In 1602 he had aided in sending Captain Gosnold
for the exploration of the New England coast; in
1605 he had furnished with others the moneys for
the voyage of Captain Weymouth. Of the Council
for Virginia Southampton became a member in 1609.
Sandys had been a member since 1607. Opposed to
the growing imperialism of the King, his pretensions
to divine right, his religious and political intolerance,
and the intrigues of his tools—the Spanish or Court
party—in the company, these and other statesmen
moved for charters for Virginia by which the more
dangerous prerogatives of James I should pass to
the body politic, and by which ultimately the colonists should compass an independent development.

[1] Alexander Brown, English Politics in Early Virginia History,
6-7; Genesis of the United States, I, 52-63, Letters Patent of Apr.
1606; 65-75, Articles, Instructions and Orders of Nov. 1606;
also J. A. Doyle, English Colonies in America, vol. 1, ch. vi.

Burdened neither by autocracy nor communism, they were to be secure in the individual enjoyment of prosperity and of civil and religious liberty. At home the Patriots had suffered from despotism both of church and state; "in Virginia they purposed to erect," as Sir Edwin Sandys announced, "a free, popular state, in which the inhabitants should have no government putt upon them but by their own consente." [1] These Patriots were men with whom Shakespeare spake; and that he was in sympathy with the ideals of the party and in confidential relation with some of its leaders we shall presently see. That we may have before us the questions at issue let us run rapidly over the course of the conflict during his lifetime and that of his immediate contemporaries.

By a charter obtained in 1609, through the efforts of the Patriots, the London Company for Virginia acquired many of the powers heretofore vested in the crown. The political control of the colony passed in a significant degree to the body politic of planters and adventurers. Though the planters gained no significant liberties, the corporation gained many; and the company as a whole became democratic in organization. [2] By a third charter, in 1612, the Patriots acquired for the company still further

[1] Brown, Eng. Pol. in Va. Hist., 8, 11, 47.

[2] Brown, Genesis, I, 206–237, The Second Charter; 259–277, New Britain (showing the ideals of the Council). See also H. L. Osgood, The American Colonies in the Seventeenth Century, 56–59.

powers of self-direction and of dealing with the laziness, insubordination, and crime due in larger part to the still existing joint-stock provisions stipulated by the King's first charter. Soon steps were taken for the abandonment of the system of communal proprietorship: individual allotments were assigned to some of the colonists; and thus were laid the foundations of personal effort and industrial prosperity. This under the governorship of the unjustly execrated Sir Thomas Dale. "With great and constant severity," says the chief founder of our colonial liberties, Sir Edwin Sandys, "with great and constant severity he reclaimed almost miraculously these idle and disordered people, and reduced them to labor and an honest fashion of life." [1]

In the year of Shakespeare's death, 1616, the joint-stock period came to an end; and the victory of the Patriots seemed to be in sight. But the King, assisted by the Court party, had meanwhile been laying plans to negative the new property rights of the colonists and utterly to defeat the aspirations of the managers. Working in collusion with certain minions of the King, Dale's successor, Argall, proceeded to obtain a patent which should turn the plantation into "a private or proprietary affair exempt from all authority to the company and the colony." The Patriot party which, as Lodge puts it, was "begin-

---

[1] For the Third Charter see Brown, Genesis, II, 540–553; for Dale, *ibid.*, II, 869–874, and H. C. Lodge, Hist. Eng. Colonies in America, 8.

ning to make the London Company for Virginia a
school for education in free government found that
the governorship of their colony had been stolen,
and the enterprise almost ruined by the court minor-
ity. The grievances of the Virginians found, therefore,
a ready hearing from men upon whom the hand of
majesty had already begun to press." [1] A revolution
in the company swept not only Argall but the King's
party out of power. Sir Edwin Sandys, the Earl
of Southampton, and others of the Patriot party
in Parliament and in the company, deriving their
authority from the liberal provisions of the charters
which they had already secured from the King,
framed for the suffering colonists a "Great Charter
or Commissions of Priviledges, Orders, and Lawes."
This was ratified by the Virginia court in London in
1618, and under its provisions was established, in
the year following, the first representative government in America. The governor's power was limited
by a general assembly consisting of a council and of
burgesses freely elected from each local group of
colonists; and this assembly had "power to make and
maintaine whatsoever lawes and orders should by
them be thought good and profitable." By this
charter—the outcome of the efforts of the Liberals
at home—the foundation was laid for constitutional
government in the New World. Government by
consent of the governed, freedom of speech, equality

[1] Lodge, Eng. Col. in Am., 8–12; Records of the Virginia Co.,
I, 65.

before the law, trial by jury were assured. And by another constitution some three years later: all immunities and franchises of English freemen were confirmed anew; and the usages of English law and English courts, and the regularity of legislative assemblage, prescribed. Provision was made for consent of the company at home to legislative enactment; but it was provided that no orders from London should be binding on the colony unless ratified by her Assembly. Upon the charters thus culminating all future rights and liberties of the colonies—north and south, of the revolutionary America of 1775 and of the Republic of today, are built.[1]

In 1619 Sandys and Southampton gained complete control of the Virginia Company; but from that time on the Patriots and the King were more than ever locked in combat. In 1624 the cause was temporarily lost. Virginia became a royal province and the charters were annulled. "But the principles that inspired" the founders of our liberty "had been planted in America. The seed had germinated, and the tender plant was growing in our free air."[2]

[1] E. Eggleston, The Beginnings of a Nation, 51–56; Lodge, Eng. Col. Am., 8–12; Brown, Eng. Pol. in Va., 29.
[2] Brown, Eng. Pol. in Va., 53.

CHAPTER II

SHAKESPEARE AND THE LIBERALS OF THE VIRGINIA COMPANY

I

OF the liberal faction in the Virginia Company, several, as I have said, were Shakespeare's friends or acquaintances; several were friends of his friends. Prominent among them was a group consisting of the Earl of Southampton, the Earl of Pembroke, and others who had been associates of the high-spirited and unfortunate Robert Devereux, Earl of Essex. If Shakespeare did not know Essex, he at any rate admired him and gave him his homage. When, between 1594 and 1596, the dramatist wrote his anti-Semitic play, The Merchant of Venice, it is not unlikely that he had in mind affairs in which Essex had vital and well-known interest. For the Christian Antonio appears to reflect the distinguished Antonio Perez, a friend of the Earl, and Shylock to be a caricature of a former protégé of Essex—the Jewish physician, Roderigo Lopez, who had been recently tried and hanged for an alleged attempt to poison not only Perez but the Queen herself.[1] This is the

---

[1] See Lee's Life of Shakespeare, p. 72, for statement and further references.

Essex, impatient of the caresses and caprices of majesty, darling of the populace, whom, as "general of our gracious Empress" in command against the Irish rebels, Shakespeare had, in 1599, celebrated in the prologue to the last act of Henry V. This is the Essex, who, failing in his Irish campaign and incurring the displeasure of Elizabeth, opened negotiations with the Puritans and the King of Scots, and finally entered into a plot for the removal of the Queen's councillors. In order to foment a popular uprising on behalf of the Earl his fellow-conspirators persuaded Shakespeare's company of players to present Richard II, a drama which with its scenes of deposition and murder had been always regarded by the Queen with suspicion, aversion. "I am Richard II," cried she afterwards, "know ye not that?" The man who "bespoke the play," Sir Charles Percy, son of the Earl of Northumberland, was familiar with Shakespeare's genius, as we see from his allusions to Silence and Justice Shallow in a letter written about a year before. The poet's tragedy was performed February 7, 1601, the night before Essex and his friends, among them the Earl of Southampton and Charles Percy, made their ill-fated march upon the palace.[1]

Essex died for his treason, and others with him. Southampton, who had already forfeited the royal

[1] See Shakesp. Allusion-Book, I, 81–3, 86–7, 98; also State Papers, Domestic, Vol. 275, No. 146; Vol. 278, Nos. 78, and 85.

favor by marrying Essex's cousin, without the
Queen's consent, and more recently by accepting
without her sanction the mastership of the Horse
in Essex's Irish expedition, was sentenced to death,
but reprieved and committed to the Tower for life.
Sir Gelly Merrick who gave the 40/ to the actors
of the Globe on that unlucky sixth of February was
of those who were beheaded; but the players themselves escaped punishment. Shakespeare kept silence. Two years later when the great Queen died,
he still kept a significant silence; nay, was reproached
that he did not "Drop from his honied muse one
sable tear To mourn her death." But his reticence
was natural. Though Elizabeth had "gracèd his
desert, And to his laies opened her royal eare,"
Essex had been his admiration and Southampton was
his benefactor and friend. To Southampton he had
dedicated his Venus and Adonis in 1593; the next
year, his Rape of Lucrece—and with what sincerity
of devotion: "The love I dedicate to your Lordship
is without end. . . . The warrant I have of your
honourable disposition, not the worth of my un-
tutor'd lines, makes it assured of acceptance. What
I have done is yours; what I have to do is yours;
having part in all I have, devoted yours. Were my
worth greater, my duty would show greater; mean-
time, as it is, it is bound to your lordship; to whom
I wish long life, still strengthened with all happiness. Your Lordship's in all duty, William Shakespeare." Sentiments of love and duty, and profes-

sion of worth inadequate to express them, repeated
distinctly in that sonnet which opens,

Lord of my love, to whom in vassalage
Thy merit hath my duty strongly knit,
To thee I send this written ambassage,
To witness duty, not to show my wit:
Duty so great, which wit so poor as mine
May make seem bare, in wanting words to show it,
But that I hope some good conceit of thine
In thy soul's thought, all naked, will bestow it.

Of the poet's sonnets of undying friendship there is
little doubt that several were addressed to the same
gracious personage, and that, conventional as their
temper and fashion may be, they express a sincere
affection. To no other literary patron than Southampton do we know that Shakespeare indited a
dedicatory epistle; and we know of no other who so
munificently assisted a poet as Southampton is
reputed to have done by Shakespeare. Even though
the gift of which tradition informs us—"a thousand
pounds to enable him to go through with a purchase"
—be exaggerated, the tradition had currency within
a hundred years of the death of both, and illustrates
the popular recognition of their friendship.

It was only after James I had mounted the throne
and liberated Shakespeare's friend "supposed as
forfeit to a confined doom" that the poet, hailing
the era of happy augury, broke silence concerning
the "eclipse of that mortal moon" Elizabeth:

Not mine own fears, nor the prophetic soul
Of the wide world, dreaming on things to come,
Can yet the lease of my true love control,
Supposed as forfeit to a confined doom.
The mortal moon hath her eclipse endured,
And the sad augurs mock their own presage;
Incertainties now crown themselves assured,
And peace proclaims olives of endless age.
Now with the drops of this most balmy time
My love looks fresh . . .
And thou in this shalt find thy monument
When tyrants' crests and tombs of brass are spent.

Ill-advised as Essex's uprising had been it was a movement directed against the increasing arbitrariness of the aged Queen, and with the purpose of establishing a more liberal plan of government and ensuring its continuance by settlement of the succession upon the King of Scots. By the public the memory of Essex was cherished: both he and his associates were acclaimed as patriots. None more so than Southampton,—and fittingly; within five years, as member of the Council for Virginia, he was heading the reformers of that company, a patriot still but with face now set against the tyrannous policy of the Stuart prince upon whose accession too many hopes had been built.

To this group belonged also William Herbert, third Earl of Pembroke, a nephew of Sir Philip Sidney whose widow Essex had married. He had been knighted by that earl at Cadiz in 1596, and had been on friendly terms with him; but he took no active part in the uprising of 1601. Pembroke was a heavy investor in the Virginia enterprise, and became a member of the Council in 1609. For fifteen years he faithfully served the interests of the colony. From 1620 on he was a member of the Council for New England as well, as was Southampton.[1] That he was acquainted with Shakespeare, not merely in his function as dramatist and actor at Court but personally, no one can question who studies the evidence without prejudice. It was to Pembroke and Pembroke's brother, Philip, the Earl of Montgomery that two of Shakespeare's most intimate friends, the editors of the first folio of Shakespeare's plays, dedicated that volume, saying that they did so because "your lordships have been pleased to think these trifles something heretofore, and have prosequuted

[1] For the records of the Virginia Company of London, the lists of adventurers, and the membership of the Councils to 1619, the most convenient authority is Alexander Brown's comprehensive and admirably documented Genesis of the United States, 2 vols., Boston, 1890. Brief but invaluable biographies of persons connected with the founding of Virginia are appended (II, 807–1068). Reference may also be made to the Abstract of Proceedings of the Virginia Company of London (Hist. Soc. Va.), the Calendar of State Papers, Domestic and Colonial, the Massachusetts Hist. Soc. Publications, E. D. Neill's Extracts from Manuscript Records of the Va. Company, and his Hist. Va. Co. of London, Doyle's English Colonies in America, and his Records of the Va. Company, Stith's History of Virginia, the entries in the Dictionary of National Biography, Wood's Athenae, Aubrey's Brief Lives, and other sources as mentioned in the text.

both them and their Authour living, with so much
favour;" and because they "hope that . . . you
will use the like indulgence toward them you have
done unto their parent." These words were written
and published in 1623, only seven years after Shakespeare's death. The writers, Heminges and Condell,
had known the dramatist for twenty years and more;
they had acted in one after another of his plays;
they had been his business partners for many years.
It was not only "these remaines of your Servant
Shakespeare" that their lordships had furthered
with their "favour," but the "parent," while he was
still living. The writers do not mean that as Lord
Chamberlain, exercising supreme authority in the-
atrical affairs, Pembroke had shown favor to Shakespeare. The favor was unofficial. For Pembroke
did not become Chamberlain till 1615, four years
after Shakespeare had practically ceased making or
acting plays, and had retired to Stratford,—in fact
when he had but four months more to live. The
period of this acquaintance and friendly relation
was during the earlier years of James's reign, when
Pembroke was a man about Court; or earlier still
when, as Lord Herbert, he used to live at Baynard's
Castle near the theatre of Blackfriars. That was
between 1598 and 1601, just the time of the Essex
and Southampton crisis to which we have recently
referred. Pembroke was a well-known friend of other
poets—of Donne and George Herbert and Vaughan:
and he had been from 1602, especially from 1610,

on, a "learned and most noble patron of learning"—
of Jonson, Chapman and William Browne, and many
more. Now he was Chamberlain as well. It was
therefore doubly reasonable that Heminges and
Condell should turn to him for patronage when they
were issuing the folio of their fellow-player's works.
The patronage they solicited was, however, not
for Shakespeare but for themselves as editors; and
the justification they alleged was not that Pembroke had ever been the formal literary patron of
Shakespeare as of Jonson and the rest, but that
Pembroke and his brother had expressed their
"likings of the severall parts, when they were acted,"
and had used "indulgence" to the dramatist.

"There is great difference," say the editors, "whether
a Booke choose his Patrones or find them: This hath
done both." Shakespeare had done the finding.
That Heminges and Condell should, in the choosing,
associate with the Lord Chamberlain his brother,
a distinguished nobleman, to be sure, but not patron
of letters, needs no explanation but that given: he
also had, not formally but personally, "prosequuted"
the "Authour living with much favour." The personal acquaintance of Pembroke and Shakespeare
would probably never have been questioned had it
not been for the untenable contention advanced by
some that Pembroke, Lord William Herbert, was
more than an acquaintance—no other than the "W.
H.," the "onlie begetter" of Shakespeare's Sonnets.
To make a clean sweep of all this, the over-zealous

have emptied out the baby with the bath. For our present purpose the plain statement of Heminges and Condell is enough. Like Pembroke, the Earl of Montgomery was in 1609 a subscriber to the Virginia Company. He became member of the Council under the third charter, 1612; and as late as 1643, having cast his lot with Parliament against the crown, he is, with Pym and Cromwell, one of the commissioners appointed for the liberal government of the plantations in America.

Three other adherents of the Essex group in the Council—Sir Robert Sidney, Sir Henry Neville and Lord De la Warr—were familiar with various friends of Shakespeare. Sidney, the brother of the matchless Sir Philip, was Pembroke's uncle; and with the Earl of Essex he had been knit by ties of affection as well as of family. He was created councillor for Virginia in the same year as Pembroke; and, as a liberal, he stood shoulder to shoulder with Southampton in the battles of the company till its dissolution in 1624. He shared also the latter Earl's love of poetry and of poets. To him in the Essex days of 1599, Southampton is sending "certain songs" that he may share his delight in them. As Baron Penshurst in 1603, and afterward as Lord Lisle, Sidney threw open his home at Penshurst to the poets—Ben Jonson and many another friend of Shakespeare. That the Sidney and Shakespeare of this circle of common acquaintance did not know each other is, to say the least, unlikely.

The interests and intimacies of Shakespeare and Henry Neville, of Billingbear in Berkshire, coincided in half a dozen different ways. Another of Essex's knights of Cadiz, Sir Henry had participated in the Earl's conspiracy of 1601, had been convicted of treason, thrown into the Tower with Southampton, and held there till the accession of James I. He was for years a close companion of Shakespeare's devoted panegyrist, Hugh Holland, and of Holland's friend, Christopher Brooke, another of Shakespeare's personal admirers. He was an excellent patron of poets, this Sir Henry—of Davies of Hereford, Ben Jonson, Beaumont, and Fletcher, all well known to Shakespeare. His name is to be seen scribbled over the fly-leaf of a manuscript of "Mr. Frauncis Bacon's" essays and speeches (about 1597) together with those of Bacon (a relative) and Shakespeare: authorities say, by Davies of Hereford, the friend of all three. Neville was early interested in the Virginia enterprise, a member of the council from 1607 till his death in 1615, and one of its Patriots and a leader of the Independent party in Parliament. His independence, indeed, prevented him, in 1612, from becoming Secretary of State. His son and successor, of the same name, was a subscriber to the Plantation in 1611; and one of the daughters, Elizabeth, married a brother of Sir William Berkeley, afterwards Governor of Virginia.

Thomas West, third Lord De la Warr. whom I have mentioned as of the Essex group, had taken part with them in the uprising of 1601 and been imprisoned therefor. A member, since 1609, of the Virginia Council, he remained always a close political ally of Southampton, Pembroke, Neville, and other old friends of Essex. While he was governing Virginia in 1610–11, we find his younger brother, John, habitually frequenting a select and convivial dining club in company with Shakespeare's friends, Christopher Brooke and Hugh Holland. But of that later. In the history of Virginia Lord De la Warr plays a critical role. If it had not been for his arrival in the nick of time "before Algarnoone Fort the sixt of June," 1610, with reinforcements and supplies, the colony would have been abandoned by Gates and his party. And for this reason, if no other, the claim made for De la Warr—"If any man can be called the founder of Virginia he is the man" [1] —may be justified. Though empowered to rule by martial law of draconic severity, his short period of office was on the whole beneficial, and his services were acknowledged by the colonists as well as by the authorities at home.

The Sir Thomas Gates whom I have just mentioned forms a significant link between Shakespeare and the affairs of the Virginia Company. Though we have no testimony concerning his immediate acquaintance with Shakespeare we know that they had associations and informations in common. Gates, like Pembroke and Neville, was a knight of

[1] Gen. U. S., II, 1049.

the Essex creation and supporter of the liberal faction in the Virginia Company. With his adventures in the New World in 1609–10 Shakespeare was extraordinarily familiar. In The Tempest, written soon afterward, he makes use of minute details of Gates's shipwreck off Bermuda in 1609, of his life on the island, and of his experiences as lieutenant-general and administrator of Virginia. Of these details some, as we shall presently see, were derived from a confidential account set down in the colony, brought over to England by Gates, and not made public for years after Shakespeare's death. Sir Thomas was one of the original incorporators in 1606 under the first charter for Virginia, and was member of the council under the second, in 1609. The next year he became the "first sole and absolute governor of the colony;" and from the middle of 1611 till April, 1614, he was again the ranking officer. Of him, five years later, Sir Edwin Sandys said, "Sir Thomas Gates had the Honour to all posterity of being the first named in his Majesty's Patent and Grant of Virginia, and was also the first that by his wisdom, Industry, and Valour, accompanied with exceeding Pains and Patience in the Midst of many Difficulties, had laid the foundation of the present prosperous State of the Colony."[1] In November, 1620, King James appointed Gates one of the "first moderne and present Councill established at Plymouth, in the county of Devon,

[1] Brown, Genesis, II, 894; Records of the Virginia Co., I, 21.

for the planting, ruling, ordering, and governing of New England in America."

II

Other liberals of the Virginia Company impinge upon Shakespeare's orbit, who were not distinctively of the Essex provenience. Some of them knew him. Others knew of him and probably were acquainted with him, for they were personally connected with his friends among poets, playwrights, or actors,—or with those who paid contemporary tribute to his personality and genius. This group we may style the legal-literary. First to be mentioned are Christopher Brooke of Lincoln's Inn and John Selden of the Inner Temple. The former, of the Virginia Council from 1609, was a powerful member of the company until its dissolution. The latter was a member of the company after the adoption of the third charter and an adviser in legal affairs. With Selden Brooke drafted several of the liberal codes of law and government for Virginia. In Parliament, on more than one occasion, the two friends withstood the King's interference with the affairs of the corporation. They were both, in their hours of ease, poets after a fashion, members of the pastoral coterie of the Inns of Court; and one of their most cherished protégés in that coterie was William Ferrar, the younger son of Nicholas, at whose house the Virginia Courts were held for many years.

Brooke's bosom friend was the poet, Donne. He was also intimate with Shakespeare's fellow-dramatists, Jonson and Drayton, and his epigrammatic admirer, Davies of Hereford; and he was thoroughly versed in the business affairs of Shakespeare's corporation, for he acted as advocate for certain proprietors of the Blackfriars theatre at a time when the poet was still one of the seven shareholders. That was in 1612. The two shareholders involved were Shakespeare's old friends and fellow-players, Burbage and Heminges. The case was a bill of complaint brought before the Court of Chancery by one Kirkham for recovery of profits in the Blackfriars playhouse. Brooke was one of several barristers engaged; but the records show that he played a very important part in having the "plaintiff's bill clearly and absolutely dismissed out of this courte." [1] Two years later this professional adviser and confidant of Shakespeare's partners published a poem called The Ghost of Richard III, in which he not only paraphrased and quoted lines from the poet's Richard III, but paid "graceful tribute" to Shakespeare himself. "To him that impt my fame," says Brooke's Ghost of Richard,

> To him that impt my fame with Clio's quill,
> Whose magick rais'd me from oblivion's den;
> That writ my storie on the Muses' hill,
> And with my actions dignifi'd his pen:

[1] Greenstreet Papers, VIII, in ~~Fleery~~, Hist. Stage, 250.

He that from Helicon sends many a rill,
Whose nectared veins are drunke by thirstie men;
 Crown'd be his stile with fame, his head with bayes;
 And none detract, but gratulate his praise.

Such whole-hearted appreciation of Shakespeare still living, of his magic, his demiurgic genius, his nectared vein,—nay, more, such generous delight in the praise that others gave him—sounds a very personal note, indeed.

"In the paper buildings" of the Inner Temple "which looke towards the garden," as Aubrey tells us, Brooke's ally in politics and poetry, John Selden, had his chambers. There he kept "a plentifull table and was never without learned company." Of that company were Shakespeare's Jonson and Drayton—frequently, as we know. And of it too, we may reasonably surmise, were their loving disciples, Beaumont and Fletcher. For the former was of the Inner Temple himself, and in 1613, its poet and masque-maker; and the latter was of Selden's social and family connection. For the past four years these Castor and Pollux dramatists had been writing plays for Shakespeare's company at Court and the Globe and Blackfriars; and in 1613 Fletcher was engaged in the completion of Shakespeare's Henry VIII.

That Shakespeare knew Sir Dudley Digges, another legal and literary patriot of the Virginia Council, we may be practically certain. There was never a more devoted worshipper of the poet in the flesh and spirit than Sir Dudley's brother, Leonard. The lad was twenty-one when Dudley joined the Council, and but twenty-eight when Shakespeare died. Of that death no contemporary has written with more abiding sense of personal loss. His verses for the Folio of 1623, To the Memorie of the deceased Authour, are addressed not to a name but to a man whom alive he had viewed and honored and whom he misses:

Shakespeare, at length thy pious fellowes give
The world thy Workes; thy Workes by which out-live
Thy Tombe, thy name must; when that stone is rent
And Time dissolves thy Stratford moniment,
Here we alive shall view thee still. This Booke,
When Brasse and Marble fade, shall make thee looke
Fresh to all Ages . . . .
Nor shall I e're beleeve, or thinke thee dead—
Though mist—untill our bankrout Stage be sped
(Impossible) with some new strain t' out-do
Passions of Juliet and her Romeo.

And in another tribute, written before 1635, and prefixed to the edition of Shakespeare's Poems issued in 1640, it is the memory of the man Shakespeare that he cherishes—

Poets are born not made: when I would prove
This truth, the glad remembrance I must love
Of never-dying Shakespeare, who alone
Is argument enough to make that one.

Nor has anyone borne more convincing testimony to the poet's originality and ease of composition, and his unquestioned authorship of the plays eulogized—Julius Cæsar, Othello, Henry IV, Much Ado, and Twelfth Night—and to their supreme popularity when acted upon the stage in Shakespeare's day, and when Leonard was spectator of the "ravish'd Audience." The Diggeses came of an academic and literary family. That in the little world of Iacobean London Sir Dudley, himself a scholar, diplomat and author, did not know the beloved idol of his brother is inconceivable.

Sir Dudley was an ardent devotee to the advancement of the Virginia and Bermuda enterprises from his appointment to the Council in 1609 to the day of his death in 1639. He was in close touch with Southampton, Brooke and Selden; and in Charles I's reign, with Edward Sackville, the Ferrars, and other liberals, he still strove to regain for the colony the privileges which had made it for a time practically self-governing. Two of Digges's sons were likewise concerned. The younger, Edward, having settled in Virginia, preserved there the patriotic tradition of the family, and during the Commonwealth was one of those three Puritan governors, elected by the Assembly of Virginia, under whom the colony enjoyed its most prosperous days, its most independent administration, and its fullest measure of popular rights.

With more than one of the Essex group of the Virginia Council and the legal-literary group, it is easy to link Sir Edward Sackville, later, fourth Earl of Dorset. The Sackvilles, Fletchers and Seldens were allied by intermarriage. To Shakespeare's Jonson and Drayton Sir Edward was a kindly patron; and of Southampton, Pembroke and Brooke he was a loyal colleague in the promotion of the colony in and after 1612. When the King was wrecking the Virginia Company in 1622–24, Sackville resisted with Southampton and Sandys; and, though a cavalier under Charles I, he remained till his death, in 1652, a supporter of the rights of Virginia.

III

An amusing set of macaronic Latin verses, entitled *Mr. Hoskins, his Convivium Philosophicum,*[1] written between 1608 and 1611, enlarges our purview of the social world in which some of Shakespeare's friends of the Virginia Company moved. We catch here a glimpse of a very genial club to which belonged no fewer than nine of the liberal promoters of the Virginia enterprise. The membership numbered twelve—lawyers, statesmen, patrons of letters, poets, architects, travellers, country knights and squires; and the usual place of dining was the Mitre Inn close by the Inns of Court. The building still stands at the top of Mitre Court, a few yards back from the thoroughfare of Fleet Street.

[1] Printed by A. Clark in his Aubrey's Brief Lives, II, 50–51. See also Cal. State Papers (Dom.), Sept. 2, 1611; and C. M. Gayley, Francis Beaumont, Dramatist, 146–149.

The Latin invitation to the symposium, as translated by a contemporary, opens—

> Whosoever is contented
> That a number be convented,
>   Enough but not too many;
> The *Miter* is the place decreed—
> For witty jests and cleanly feed,
>   The betterest of any;

and the author proceeds to rehearse the names and characteristics of the jolly souls "convented." Among them we recognize at once Christopher Brooke, his chamber-fellow of Lincoln's Inn, John Donne, and Sir Henry Neville; also Hugh Holland of the Mermaid Club, who wrote a few years later the tearful sonnet on Shakespeare's death, beginning,

> Those hands, which you so clapt, go now, and wring
> You Briteines brave; for done are Shakespeare's dayes:
> His dayes are done, that made the dainty Playes,
> Which make the Globe of heav'n and earth to ring;

and ending,

> For though his line of life went soone about,
> The life yet of his lines shall never out.

Not only had Shakespeare such a nucleus of association, personal or literary, and already ascertained, in the club, most of the commensals were in close touch with his friends in town or country. Four of them were of the Virginia Council: Brooke, Neville,

Sir Robert Phillips—appointed in 1614, a supporter of Southampton and Sandys, a leader of the popular party in Parliament, imprisoned by James I in 1622 —and Richard Martin, a learned Bencher of the Middle Temple and friend of Selden. Martin was much interested in dramatic pageantry: in 1613, one of the "undertakers" of that "Memorable Maske" for the marriage of the Princess Elizabeth, in which the chief actors posed as Virginian priests and princes. He was a friend of its author, George Chapman, variously connected in literature and life with Shakespeare and closely with Ben Jonson. Of the regular drama as well Martin was a patron, and more especially of that written by his "true lover" Jonson. Together the twain used to frequent the merry meetings of the poets at the Mermaid in Bread Street. An opponent of monopolies under Queen Elizabeth, Martin was always a liberal. He joined the Virginia Company in 1609, became member of the council in 1612, and in 1614 made a speech before Parliament in support of the policy of the Earl of Southampton, Lord De la Warr and other proponents of Virginian liberties that is not yet forgotten. He ripped up the procrastinating and disorderly procedure of Parliament with such temerity and scorn that it required all the skill of his fellows in the Virginia Council and the Mitre Club to extricate him from the consequences.[1]

Of the Mitre fellowship five other convivial souls

[1] For the outline see Neill, Va. Co. of London, 68-72.

were "adventurers" in the Virginia enterprise, though not members of the council. One of them, John Hoskins, a serjeant of the Middle Temple, had joined the Virginia Company in 1611. In 1614 we find him, also, asserting the cause of popular rights as against the favoritism of the king with such spirit in Parliament that he is given a chance to cool his ardor in the tower. Beloved of Brooke, Holland and Martin and of the dramatists and poets of their circle and Shakespeare's, he was of "excellent witt" that commended him "to all ingeniose persons," and an incomparable writer of drolleries. He is the Mr. Hoskins to whom, as we have seen above, the macaronic invitation to this "symposiaque" at the Mitre is attributed. Another of those "convented" was Richard Connock, or Conyoke, a member of Parliament, a supporter of Walter Raleigh and an "adventurer" of 1612. A third was John West, younger brother to Lord De la Warr, first governor of Virginia. Settling, later, in the colony, West became himself governor in 1635, and died there. Of his descendants many have been distinguished in the history of this country. A fourth was John Donne. An adherent of Essex in 1596–7, his political, literary, and social affiliations were in half a dozen ways interwoven with those of Shakespeare. With the Virginia Company he was first formally connected in 1622; and in that year, as "Brother of this Companie and of their Counsell," and Dean of St. Paul's, he preached their annual sermon. With rare beauty and prophecy he alludes to "the great work performed in the beginning of a Church and Commonwealth in America, where their children could be well accommodated, and adds that those that were young would live to see that 'You have made this Island, which is but the suburbs of the Old World, a bridge, a gallery to the New; to join all to that world that shall never grow old, the Kingdom of Heaven.'" [1] Last of these Mitre Club subscribers to the colonial venture, a lifelong friend of Donne and Brooke, celebrated by Ben Jonson and acquainted from youth up with that other intimate of Shakespeare, Drayton, was Sir Henry Goodere of Polesworth in Warwickshire. His uncle, of the same name, also of Polesworth, had been "the first cherisher of Drayton's muse," and our Sir Henry had married one of the Polesworth cousins, the "Panape" of Drayton's verse. The family of Goodere had fallen under the royal disfavor in Elizabeth's earlier days; and, apparently, Sir Henry the younger had been an Essex sympathizer. He was with the Earl in Ireland and was there knighted by him, in 1599. His name appears among those of subscribers to the Virginia enterprise in the list of 1611.

IV

The mention of the Gooderes and of Warwickshire reminds us that, in the immediate neighborhood of

[1] Neill, Virginia Company of London, 361-2.

Stratford, Shakespeare had several acquaintances who were prominent investors in the Virginia under- taking. Since 1597, Shakespeare had been the master of New Place in his native town. As the bearer of a coat of arms, and as proprietor after 1601 of large holdings in the neighborhood of Strat- ford, he had become one of the landed gentry. From 1601 on he spent part of every year at New Place: and about 1611, though still maintaining certain relations with his old partners in London, he made it his permanent abode.[1] Of the neighboring county families one of the best known to him was that of Clifford Chambers, an ancient and beautiful seat, about two miles across the fields from Stratford, in Gloucestershire. There was much talk at Clifford about the Virginia plantation: for, during Shake- speare's later years. Sir Henry Rainsford, lord of the manor, was a member of the company. He was a member of the council, too, perhaps as early as 1613, certainly by 1617-18. We find him further investing in the corporation as late as 1620, when he bought shares of his fellow-councillor, Sir Thomas Gates;[2] and again in the following year he added to his shares. Lady Rainsford was both cousin and sister- in-law of the Sir Henry Goodere whom we met in the Mitre Club. She is the Anne Goodere, the "flower of womanhood" of Drayton's youthful homage,—the divine "Idea" to whom through life

[1] Sir Sidney Lee, Life of Shakespeare (ed. 1915), 450.
[2] Gen. U. S., II, 797, 975.

he is "still inviolate." Rainsford, himself, "Past all degrees that was so dear to me" is Drayton's exemplar of "what a friend should be." Clifford Manor was Drayton's yearly resort in summer: for him "Many a time the Muses' quiet port." And near by was his fellow dramatist's hospitable New Place, where, according to a story handed down by a contemporary of Drayton and Jonson, Shakespeare entertained those two old friends at a "merry meeting," shortly before his death.

Shakespeare's son-in-law, Dr. John Hall of Old Town, Stratford, was the Rainsfords' family physician. He once cured Drayton while at Clifford of a " tertian," and he records in his observation book the "syrup of violets" that he prescribed for the "excellent poet." About 1600, Dr. Hall is attending Lady Rainsford after childbirth; and describing her as "near 27, beautiful and of a gallant structure of body." On other pages of his notebook are entered curious and somewhat repellent recipes with which from time to time he relieved her ailments; and he is still attending her as late as 1634.[1] Not only through Hall and Drayton is the personal intercourse of Shakespeare and Rainsford assured for us, but through the family of Combe at Stratford, long standing acquaintances and good friends of both the dramatist and the lord of Clifford Manor. When in 1613, John Combe made his will, Sir Henry

---

[1] Dr. John Hall's Select Observations, London, 1679; pp. 18, 134, 158 (Obs. LXVIII).

Rainsford of Clifford Chambers was an overseer of it "receiving 5*l.* for his service, while Lady Rainsford was allotted 40*s.* wherewith to buy a memorial ring." And "to Mr. William Shakespeare he left five pounds." [1] It is interesting to note this coupling of the names of Rainsford and Shakespeare in the year when the latter was having his comedy of Bermudan and Virginian allusion revived at Court, and about the time when the former was allying himself with the Virginia Company. Interesting, too, to recall that both Jonson and Drayton had written their names into the literary history of Virginia some seven or eight years earlier. But of that presently.

The circle in which the Combes, Rainsfords, and the master of New Place moved included various county families about Stratford: prominent among these—the Verneys and the Grevilles. Of the Verneys, one, Sir Richard of Compton Verney, was an executor of the testamentary document mentioned above. And Verney's brother-in-law, Sir Fulke Greville, later Lord Brooke, the political philosopher, statesman, and poet, was the friend of more than one of Shakespeare's associates and the patron of some. Davies of Hereford, who records at one time his admiration of Shakespeare, records but a few years later his admiration of Shakespeare's neighbor Greville; [2] and to Greville, in whose household he

[1] Lee, Life of Shakespeare (ed. 1915), 471.
[2] Microcosmos, 1603, p. 215; and a sonnet to Greville, written before 1609, in the Scourge of Folly (1610), p. 194.

lived as a page, Davenant, Shakespeare's young friend, and probably godson, acknowledged his deep indebtedness. Greville's estate of Beauchamp Court, Alcester, was but nine miles from Stratford. During the period, moreover, of Shakespeare's residence at New Place, Stratford, Greville was Recorder of the borough, and justice of the peace, paid frequent visits to the town, was entertained by its officials, and knew everyone of importance there.[1] Shakespeare and he were not far apart in years, and they had interests as well as acquaintances in common. Though diverse in method and purpose of literary creativity, in some fields of poetic taste they were at one; and one idol of poetry—Sir Philip Sidney—both worshipped. In political outlook they differed sometimes in choice of protagonist and means, but generally they saw eye to eye. The charm and promise of Essex they both celebrated, and in his downfall both were afflicted. Of that "gallant young Earl," as he calls him, Greville was not only lover but kinsman; and he had lived at Essex House for the seven years preceding the Earl's arrest. The revolt he deplored; but he contended that Essex was innocent of treasonable intention and attributed his death to the machination of self-seeking flatterers of the Queen.[2] The Queen herself, Greville, unlike Shakespeare, consistently

---

[1] Lee, Life of Sh., pp. 467–8.
[2] The Life of Sir Philip Sidney in Lord Brooke's Works (ed. Grosart), 1870, Vol. IV, 157–161.

glorified, for he regarded her policy as the only bulwark of monarchical government. That he was no absolutist, however—on the contrary, a liberal or constitutional monarchist—his writings and his political career fully attest.

Here again our dramatist comes into touch with a leader in the Virginia movement. For Greville was a member of the Royal Council for the plantation as early as 1607, probably representing the second, or northern, colony; and of the London company, we know that he was a member in 1617.[1] That, under James, Greville should have favored the "Court" or "Spanish" party is impossible. As far back as 1584, with his kinsman and dear friend, Sir Philip Sidney, and with Sir Francis Drake, he had coöperated in the memorable scheme for colonizing America with English protestants in order to check the power of Spain and Rome. These projectors of the "first propounded voyage to America," as Greville, in his Life of Sidney, calls it, wise in advance of their age, would have established there an abiding and extending plantation: "an emporium for the confluence of all nations that love or profess any kind of virtue or commerce. . . . To the nobly ambitious the fayre stage of America to win honour in. To the religious divines, besides a new apostolicall calling of the last heathen to the Christian faith, a large field of reducing poor Christians, misled by the idolatry of Rome, to their

[1] Brown, Gen. U. S., I, 93; II, 906.

mother primitive Church. To the ingenuously industrious, variety of natural richesses, for new
mysteries and manufactures to work upon. To the
merchant, with a simple people, a fertile and inex-
hastible earth. To the fortune-bound, liberty. To
the curious, a fruitfull womb of innovation." [1]
Greville's retirement to private life for the eleven
years succeeding Elizabeth's death is accounted for
by dissatisfaction with the arbitrary trend of James's
rule. "The further I went," says he, "the more
discomfortable I found those new revolutions of
time" [2]—revolutions, as we have seen, increasingly
subversive not only of domestic but colonial liberty.
Of these years the last four were those that offered
Shakespeare and Greville most chance for neigh-
borly intercourse. While Chancellor of the Ex-
chequer, during the seven years which began with
1614, Greville must have sympathized with the
policy of Southampton, Sandys, and their fellow-
patriots. "The high waies of ambitious Governours," he writes, "hasten to their own desolation
and ruin." He scorns the "misgoverned courts of
princes." The root of despotic authority is "the
lavish giving away your own liberties." Among
the dissentients, headed by Robert Rich, Earl of
Warwick, who conspired in 1623 to surrender the
charter rights of the colony to the King, his name
does not appear. After his death the connection

[1] Lord Brooke's Works, Vol. IV, 118–19.
[2] Works, IV, 215.

of his family with the American plantations continued.   His cousin, the second Lord Brooke, assisted in the colonization of Connecticut.

·   Only one of Greville's works, the tragedy of Mus-
tapha, was published in his day or Shakespeare's.
But here, as in his political treatises, we find much
that resembles Shakespeare's sanity of view: the
rejection of the divine sanction of kings, and of that
oligarchical tyranny to which the "style of optimates
and democracy" alike tends; the insistence upon
constitutional monarchy sustained by law and administered by wise men in due degree of merit and
fitness; the recognition of the frailty and pathos of
humanity, but likewise of the wisdom and mercy
of a higher power.   Greville's religion takes refuge
not in an appointed ecclesiastical discipline but in a
church invisible—"of the spirit only, choosing spiritual heirs."   Such, if Shakespeare had anywhere
formulated his sovereign tolerance, would, we may
imagine, have been his solution, too.

V

In the ten years beginning with 1606 the Virginia
Council was not at any one time large in numbers.
In 1607 there were thirty-nine councillors; and we
have found that at least three of them moved in
Shakespeare's London circle, Sir Edwin Sandys,
Sir Henry Neville and Sir Fulke Greville,—the last,
as we have seen, of his immediate Warwickshire
circle as well.   In the reconstituted Council of 1609

(fifty members in all) there appear the names of three whom Shakespeare personally knew, the Earl of Southampton, the Earl of Pembroke, and Christopher Brooke—intimates of one or another of those already mentioned. Beside these there were in that council Sir Dudley Digges (whose brother "loves the glad remembrance of never-dying Shakespeare," "cannot think him dead"), Lord Lisle, Lord De la Warr and Sir Thomas Gates, all of whom spoke with friends of Shakespeare among the great, the learned and the poetic, at every turn. Of the fifteen councillors added in 1612, Philip Herbert, Earl of Montgomery, had distinguished the "Authour living" with his favor, and Richard Martin was intimate with many of his legal and literary friends. Between 1612 and the time of Shakespeare's death about eighteen new councillors were appointed: one of them without doubt well and familiarly known by Shakespeare, his neighbor of Clifford Chambers, Sir Henry Rainsford. In short, of the eighty-five members of the council during the ten years preceding Shakespeare's death—persons of political and financial importance, engaged in an unusually serious enterprise, and in frequent consultation—at least seven were men with whom Shakespeare had personal intercourse. And of six more it may be said that, to avoid hearing him mentioned with admiration or affection by their fellow-councillors, they must have stopped their ears, and that, to avoid meeting him in the company of their associates, they must have turned the corner sharp. Of the stockholders not members of the council, at least five—Selden, Hoskins, Sir Edward Sackville, John Donne, and Sir Henry Goodere—had relations especially intimate with men of letters and of public note who were Shakespeare's intimates as well.

The names given above are merely a finger-post to the ramifications of Shakespeare's acquaintance with the personnel of the Virginia Company. The lists of subscribers, whether councillors or ordinary adventurers, so far as published, include a thousand or more names. Doubtless there are many others recorded but unpublished. There were, moreover, some seventy city companies interested; but the names of the subscribing members are in only a few instances accessible in print. Scholars who have access to documents in the Public Record office, the muniments of city corporations, and other English archives are in a position to supplement the roll. I am sure that some such will show that I have but touched the fringes of the subject. For the general public, too, the Virginia undertaking was at times the absorbing topic.[1] The name of

---

[1] The Mr. Warden Field under whose hand the "Declaration of the present estate of the English in Virginia, with the final resolucon of the Great Lotterye intended for their supply" was entered at Stationers' Hall, March 9, 1614, was the Richard Field who in 1593 printed the first edition of Shakespeare's Venus and Adonis. He was from Stratford, the son of Henry Field, one of the assessors of the estate of Shakespeare's father in 1601.

those who, from all parts of the realm, took chances in the great lotteries of 1612 and 1614–15, is legion. With how many sanguine adventurers of this class Shakespeare conversed, we shall never know.

CHAPTER III

THE TEMPEST, AND AN UNPUBLISHED LETTER FROM VIRGINIA

EVEN if Shakespeare had not personally known any of the promoters of the Virginia enterprise, it is impossible that he should have been unacquainted with, or unsympathetic toward, the movement for liberty in the New World as at home. In his sonnets, and in plays written before the first settlement in Virginia, he had, as will in due course be more fully shown, put forward ideas similar to those which the Patriots sought to realize—ideas of legally constituted authority as opposed to divine right, of monarchical responsibility, of aristodemocratic government, of individual freedom and political duty, of equality before the law, of justice, fraternal effort and allegiance. His attitude in the earlier historical plays toward the problem of political coöperation is maintained in the Troilus and Cressida, written in 1602 and published with additions in 1609, and in the Coriolanus, written the latter part of 1608 or the beginning of 1609. The attitude is in all vital respects the same as that adopted by Sir Edwin Sandys, when in 1609 he drafted the petition for a charter that should make of Virginia a self-governing body politic. The political philosopher and statesman was attempting to put into practice the golden mean between tyranny and communism. Shakespeare, whose philosophy is of observation and imagination, was by no means oblivious of recorded political provenience as well. In the checks and disasters of Troilus and Cressida, he was portraying the chaos that ensues when political "degree" is suffocated. In the civil disorders of Coriolanus, he was portraying the ruin that impends when government wanders from the golden mean, and aristocratic arrogance and plebeian turbulence clash. The reform that Sandys was seeking to make concrete in a New World, Shakespeare, though with no reference to America, as yet, was implying poetically in "the weal of the common" founded in ordered service, justice, and patriotism.

In May, 1609, the efforts of Sandys and his associates of the Liberal party in the Virginia Company and Council were rewarded with initial success: a charter containing the embryo of liberties apparently unassailable by royal prerogative had been secured from King James. Shakespeare's interest in the historic as well as the romantic significance of colonial events during the next two years is writ large in the comedy which he first put upon the boards toward the end of that period. To those who inquire minutely and impartially into the sequence of events, this comedy of The Tempest will reveal also a definite acquaintance on the part of the poet with particulars unpublished at the time, and filed away in manuscript by the inner circle of the Virginia Council.

I

In June, 1609, a fleet "of seven good ships and two pinnaces" set out from Plymouth for Virginia, keeping till the twenty-third "in friendly consort together." But on the twenty-fourth came up "a most dreadfull Tempest" and drove the Sea-Venture—with Sir George Somers, admiral, and Sir Thomas Gates, the newly appointed governor of Virginia, and, worse still, with the newly granted charter, aboard—out of its course upon the rocks of the "dangerous and dreaded Ilands of the Bermuda . . . supposed to be given over to Devils and wicked Spirits." The rest of the fleet made Virginia but found things in fearful condition with the little settlement there. By the end of the year they began to return to England, vessel after vessel, with news of the loss of the Sea-Venture, and "laden with nothing but bad reports and letters of discouragement." In May of 1610, however, the shipwrecked party of Gates and Somers, having found life after all not so intolerable in the gentle climate of Bermuda, made its way in pinnaces built of cedar to Jamestown. Gates found his colony on its last legs as the result of faction, improvidence, and disease, and was about to abandon the enterprise, when Lord De la Warr arrived from England with provisions requisite for present needs and with authority to rectify the evils which had brought the plantation almost to fiasco. Sailing for a fresh stock of cattle on the fifteenth of July, Gates reached England in September, 1610. In May, 1611, he made again the outward voyage to Virginia.

Not only the Virginia Company, all England, was agog with the adventures of the returning mariners. Their stories were passed from mouth to mouth. Broadsides and pamphlets issued from the press; and letters from Virginia, some to the company in general and some to interested individuals, furnished the patentees with special information sometimes so discouraging that the council did its best to hush it up.

From one or more of these sources any playwright might have derived the hint of a play to be called The Tempest, suggestions for the dramatization of a shipwreck, incidents appropriate to life on a Devils' Island, its magical atmosphere, and reflections to be put into the mouths of the actors. Shakespeare's comedy was written after the return of Sir Thomas Gates in September, 1610; and, according to evidence generally accepted by scholars and most convincing, it was performed at Whitehall, the night of November 1, 1611. This evidence was first published in 1842 by Peter Cunningham in his Extracts from the Accounts of the Revels at Court in the reigns of Queen Elizabeth and James I, from the Original Office Books of the Masters and Yeomen—"By the

Kings Players: Hallomas nyght was presented att
Whithall before the Kinges Majestie a play called
the Tempest." Recent investigations (by Mr. Ernest
Law) of a minute, scientific, and technical kind
indicate that Cunningham's lists of plays are genuine portions of the original manuscripts. As early
as 1809, moreover, the honest and careful Edmund
Malone,[1] who had access to the documents before
Cunningham was born, has said of The Tempest:
"As I know that it had 'a being and a name' in the
Autumn of 1611, the date of the play is fixed and
ascertained with uncommon precision, between the
end of the year 1610 and the Autumn of 1611; and
it may with great probability be assigned to the
Spring of the latter year." A performance, of which
we have record, in February, 1612, may still be
thought by some, though mistakenly, to have been
the first. But whether the play first saw the light
in 1611 or in 1613 is not vital to the point which I
wish to emphasize just here. What concerns us
now is that not from oral sources alone, nor from
printed declarations, narratives, and broadsides,
accessible to the public, did Shakespeare draw the
more interesting Bermuda and Virginia informations for this play, but from a letter, jealously
guarded from the public, and accessible for long
after 1610, long after 1613, only to the inner circle
of the Virginia Company. The reader desirous of

[1] Plays and Poems of William Shakespeare (ed. 1821), XV,
423.

making an examination for himself of the sources possibly pertinent to the subject, whether in manuscript or print, during the years 1609 to 1611, or for that matter to 1613, will find a list at the end of this volume.[1]

Three pamphlets may be mentioned as summing up any printed information concerning the Virginia ventures and miscarriages that may seem to have found its way into The Tempest. Of these the first was "A True and Sincere declaration of the purpose and ends of the Plantation begun in Virginia," etc. This was entered at Stationers' Hall, December 14, 1609, "under the hands of the Treasurer and other officers of the Virginia Company." It is dated London, 1610, and is "the first tract bearing the endorsement: Set forth by the authority of the Governors and councillers established for that plantation." It was issued in order to allay the apprehensions of the public concerning the disasters of the year preceding.[2] The next was "A Discovery of the Barmudas. Otherwise called the Ile of Divels, by Sir Thomas Gates, Sir George Sommers and Captayne Newport, with divers others." This was written by one of the survivors of the wreck, Silvester Jourdan, who had returned with Gates. It is dated by the author October 13, 1610, and was published in London the same year.[3] But it does

[1] Appendix A.
[2] Reprinted in Brown, Genesis, I, 337–353.
[3] Reprinted in the 1809–12 edition of Hakluyt's Voyages, and Histories of Interesting Discoveries: A Supplement, 763–770.

not appear in the Stationers' Registers and was not
authorized by the Virginia Council. The third was
"A true Declaration of the estate of the Colony of
Virginia, with a confutacon of such scandalous
reportes as have tended to the disgrace of so worthy
an enterprise." It was entered at Stationers' Hall
on November 8, 1610, and published the same year
"by order and direction of the Councell of Virginia." [1]
The materials for this declaration are drawn partly
from Sir Thomas Gates's "Report upon Oath of
Virginia" as delivered on his return to the Council,
but not separately published, and principally from
information contained in letters received from Virginia, not published till after Shakespeare's death.

From the True and Sincere Declaration of December, 1609, mentioned above, and from a Broadside which serves as an appendix, an intending
dramatist might, if he had stopped his ears to the
subjects of public conversation, have gathered for
the first time that one of the reasons for the failure
in Virginia had been "the misgovernment"—under
the presidency of Captain John Smith—"of the
Commanders by dissention and ambition among
themselves" and "the Idlenesse and bestiall slouth
of the common sort, who were active in nothing but
adhearing to factions and parts even to their owne
ruine;" that to remedy these and similar abuses, an
expedition had been sent out under the conduct of
Sir Thomas Gates as "*one* able and absolute gov-

[1] Reprinted by Peter Force, Tracts, III, Washington: 1844.

ernor;" that "a terrible tempest" had overtaken
and "scattered the whole fleet;" that four of the
fleet had "met in consort" and made their way without "their Admiral" to Virginia; that later three
other vessels had reached harbor, but that still the
Admiral-ship was missing, with the Governor and
"all the Commissioners and principal persons
aboard." He would also learn that the rest "being
put ashore . . . no man would acknowledge a
superior nor could from this headlesse and unbridled
multitude be anything expected but disorder and
riot." The council, however, "doubts not but by
the mercy of God," the Governor "is safe, with the
Pinnace which attended him, and shall both, or are
by this time, arrived at our colony." And from the
Broadside the enquirer would learn that the "most
vile and scandalous reports, both of the Country it-
selfe, and of the Cariage of the businesse there,"
circulated at home, were attributable to "some few
of those unruly youths sent thither," who "are
come for England againe," and to "men that seeme
of the better sort, being such as lie at home, and do
gladly take all occasions to cheere themselves with
the prevention of happy successe in any action of
publike good." That "it is therefore resolved that
no . . . unnecessary person shall now be accepted,
but onely . . . sufficient, honest and good artif-
icers . . . surgeons, physitions, and learned divines."

If Shakespeare had not talked with returned

voyagers nor read other and fuller accounts than
Jourdan's narrative, the next on our list, we might
be confident that he made use of that narrative in
the composition of The Tempest.   Jourdan's Discovery was the first published account of the shipwreck of the Sea-Venture and of the ten months
spent in the Bermudas.   It is, however (as given in
Hakluyt), but a four-page quarto; and the suggestions of any possible value to a Shakespeare are
found on the first page and a half.   From none of
them should we conclude that he was dependent upon
Jourdan; for practically everything here, and much
beside pertaining to the subject, is definitely discoverable in other and better sources with which the
poet was certainly acquainted.   In the remaining
pages of Jourdan—the description of the islands,
the resumption of the voyage, and the arrival in
Virginia—there is nothing uniquely suggestive of
any feature of Shakespeare's Tempest.

The third pamphlet mentioned above, A true
Declaration of the estate of the Colony of Virginia,
covers, first, details of the storm, the wreck, the
Bermudas, and the escape (the whole summed up
as a "Tragicall-Comædie"), and, secondly, the
"testimonies of the causes of the former evils and
Sir Thomas Gates his Report upon Oath of Virginia."   The earlier sections display half a dozen
similarities in expression and three or four in thought
with Jourdan that recur in The Tempest.   But they
also narrate, in common with Shakespeare, one or

two striking particulars of the storm, of which Jourdan makes no mention. The latter part, dealing with Gates's testimony concerning Virginia, contains significant material of which Shakespeare betrays knowledge; but not Jourdan.

As I have said, the general trend of what is contained in these and other pamphlets may have reached Shakespeare by way of conversation. But the coincidences existing between The Tempest and the True Declaration alone have their common source in no publication issued at the time. Their common source was the private letter from Virginia to which I have made reference above. We find not only that much of the True Declaration which does not appear in The Tempest is drawn verbatim from that letter, but also that words, phrases, figures, incidents of The Tempest which do not appear in the True Declaration or any other printed account must, if derived from anything other than hearsay or the dramatist's imagination, have received their suggestion from that letter. And that they are not all derived from hearsay or imagination appears from the frequency of the parallelisms.

This letter, the common source of the True Declaration as a whole and of such portions of The Tempest as deal with the expedition of Sir Thomas Gates, was written by one of the survivors of the wreck, William Strachey, who according to his own statement officiated as secretary for Gates on his arrival at Jamestown and was appointed secretary and

recorder of the council in Virginia by Lord De la
Warr when, in June, 1610, he took over the governorship from Gates. Strachey's letter, sent from the
colony July 15, 1610, is addressed to an "excellent
Lady" in England. It is confidential and, from
June 2, 1609 up to the time of its despatch, describes
with vivid fidelity and unvarnished detail all the
happenings of the intervening period—discourage-
ments, mutinies and murders, factions, misgovernment, wanton sloth and waste, misery and penury,
fraud and treason, death by starvation and disease
and cruel encounter with the savages. It was not
made public till 1625, after the dissolution of the
Virginia Company. Then for the first time it saw
print in a collection known as Purchas his Pilgrimes,[1]
under the title "A true Repertory of the wracke,
and redemption of Sir Thomas Gates, Knight; upon,
and from the ilands of the Bermudas: his comming to
Virginia, and the estate of that Colonie there, and
after, under the government of the Lord La Warre,
July 15, 1610, written by William Strachey, Esquire." The chapter headings were supplied, not
by Strachey, but by the geographer and collector,
Hakluyt, who had obtained possession of the manuscript, or by Samuel Purchas, who received it from
Hakluyt and prepared it for the press. The first
chapter heading, for instance, "A most dreadfull
Tempest (the manifold deaths whereof are here to
the life described)," on the one hand contains an

[1] Edition of 1906, Vol. XIX, pp. 5–72.

editorial compliment to the author's style; on the other, is inaccurate, for there were no deaths from the tempest. The marginal notes. critical. supplementary. sometimes bombastically humorous. and with references to "our former tome," are evidently by Purchas; so also, the insertion at the end of the letter of a passage based upon A True Declaration, De la Warr's letters, and other sources. The general title also, "A True Repertory, etc.," was probably framed by Hakluyt or Purchas.

From the materials of this "Letter to an Excellent Lady" in England, which as I have said remained in manuscript till 1625, Strachey as secretary for the Council in Virginia drew up a despatch, dated Jamestown, July 7, 1610, "From the Lord De la Warr, Governor of Virginia, to the Patentees in England." It also is strictly confidential; it does not touch upon the shipwreck, but it sets forth the unhappy condition of the colony with the same frankness as the still unsent Letter to an Excellent Lady, recommends the same remedies, and as emphatically prophesies success if the remedies be adopted. The manuscript of this De la Warr despatch, preserved in the British Museum, is addressed and dated in Strachey's handwriting, and is signed by him in conjunction with De la Warr, Gates, Somers and two of the other three members of the Council. It remained in manuscript till 1849.[1]

[1] Harl. M. S. 7009, fol. 58; publ. by R. H. Major in his Introduction to The Historie of Travaile into Virginia Britannia by

From the form as printed by the Hakluyt Society we discover that nine of the thirteen pages are an almost verbatim reproduction of the Letter to an Excellent Lady. Both that letter and the despatch reached England with Sir Thomas Gates in September, 1610.

The True Declaration, which, as we have seen, Shakespeare may have read, was ready for publication in little more than a month after Gates's arrival. The compiler—for so far as the historical matter goes the pamphlet is but a restatement— had the two manuscripts mentioned above before him as he wrote. From the De la Warr Despatch he draws nothing that is not merely confirmatory of the information contained in Strachey's original "Letter;" but from that letter, afterwards published as A True Reportory, he draws much that was not repeated in the Despatch.[1] It is, indeed, surmised by some that the rough draft even of the True Declaration was prepared by Strachey himself and sent over with Gates. But the compiler, probably Sir Edwin Sandys, must have consulted Jourdan's printed Discovery as well for he embodies from it some five phrases not found in his other sources. These phrases do not recur in Shakespeare's Tempest. In fact with but one or two exceptions, which I shall presently mention, there is no

William Strachey, the First Secretary of the Colony (Hakluyt Society, 1849).
[1] See Appendix B.

similarity between Shakespeare and Jourdan that
is not also common to the True Declaration or
Strachey's Letter to an Excellent Lady. Fully
twenty passages of the Declaration are drawn verbatim or almost verbatim from the Letter, and of these
three or four reappear in The Tempest. But Shakespeare makes use as well of minute and vivid details
narrated by Strachey, of which the Declaration
makes no mention.

No other account written or printed before Hal-
lowmas, 1611 or, for that matter, February, 1613,
save Strachey's confidential letter could have furnished Shakespeare not only with certain unique
suggestions but with the sequence of verbal details
regarding the wreck, the Bermudas, and Virginia,
discoverable in The Tempest.

II

The dramatist, being a landsman and more than
ordinarily acquisitive, might have "milked some
returned mariner," as Furness has conjectured, and
Kipling contended with independent and artistic
ingenuity; but why—when he was borrowing other
hints from Strachey's letter, and with but slight
imaginative effort could turn them into something
poetically rich and strange? Several basic facts
and conceptions related not only by Strachey but
by Jourdan and the True Declaration might, indeed, have been furnished by any returned mariner:

"the dreadful storme and hideous;" the "wracke" upon the Bermudas "rent with tempests, great strokes of thunder, lightning and raine," an "inchanted place" or "pile of rockes," counted of most "no habitation for men, but rather given over to Devils and wicked Spirits;" the miraculous delivery without loss of life; the islands found "to be as habitable and commodious as most Countries of the same climate and situation," "the place itself contenting" and with "abundance by God's providence of all manner of good foode." General information of this kind might have been derived from hearsay as readily as from any manuscript or printed account. So, also, with Shakespeare's more detailed "leaky" ship and the wreck "nigh shore," which appear in all three sources; the "mariners all under hatches stow'd," who weary with "their suffer'd labour" have been "left asleep," and the "Mercy on us" from the cabin, when the ship strikes, which are suggested by Jourdan and Strachey, but not by the Declaration; the day turned into night, the "amazement" of the sea-captains and mariners, the mysterious and "fearful objects seene and heard" about the island, mentioned or suggested in the Declaration and Strachey, but not in Jourdan; the "Down with the topmast," "We split, we split," paralleled in the account of Strachey alone; the use of the term "hardly accessible," and the mention of "fairies" in the Declaration alone; the leavetaking at sea, and the temperate air of the island, implied by the others but specifically mentioned by Jourdan alone.

Such materials may have been commonplace of current report. They might have been evolved from the general reading, observation or imagination of the most modestly equipped poet. But that does not blind us to the fact that Shakespeare has transmuted particulars of which the minute and sole suggestion is to be found in Strachey's letter; and that he frequently transmutes them in the connection indicated by Strachey.

Of the tumult of the storm, Strachey says: "fury added to fury; . . . our clamours dround in the windes, and the windes in thunder. Prayers might well be in the hearts and lips, but drowned in the outcries of the Officers;" and then: "We had now purposed to have cut downe the Maine Mast." [1] In the Tempest, Shakespeare's boatswain orders "Down with the topmast," and hears *A cry within*. "A plague," he shouts, "upon this howling! They are louder than the weather or our office." Then the mariners: "All lost! To prayers! All lost!"— On the same page with "the outcries," Strachey speaks of "the glut of water;" Shakespeare too in the same sequence: "Though every drop of water . . . gape at widest to glut him:" the only appearance of that word "glut" in Shakespeare.— Shakespeare's Miranda, some ten lines further down, beseeches Prospero:

[1] Strachey, 7, 12.

If by your art, my dearest father, you have
Put the wild waters in this roar, allay them.
The sky it seems, would pour down stinking pitch,
But that the sea, mounting to the welkin's cheek,
Dashes the fire out . . . O, the cry did knock
Against my very heart!

Prospero soothes her, "Be collected; no more amazement: tell your piteous heart There's no harm done." Now, the True Declaration tells us that "the heavens were obscured, and made an Egyptian night of three daies perpetuall horror." But it was not from the Declaration, that Shakespeare drew the sequence of the roaring, the hellish pitch, the extinguishment of the fires of heaven, and Miranda's sensibility to the cry of the sufferers, her amazement; it was from the page in Strachey's letter already used and that preceding (6, 7). "A dreadful storm," says Strachey, "began to blow . . . which swelling, and roaring as it were by fits . . . at length did beat all light from heaven; which like an hell of darknesse turned blacke upon us. . . . The senses (taken up with amazement) the eares lay so sensible to the terrible cries, and murmurs of the windes, and distraction of our Company, as who was most armed, and best prepared, was not a little shaken."—Descriptions of St. Elmo's fire Shakespeare might have found in Tonson of 1555 or in a half-dozen other sources, but in none just that chrysalis of the ethereal creature "flaming amazement" who glorifies this second scene of The Tempest. The hint is in the "appari-

tion," as poetically recounted by Strachey four
pages further down—and by him alone of all historians of the Bermuda tempest—"The heavens
look'd so blacke upon us, that it was not possible
the elevation of the Pole might be observed: nor a
Starre by night, not Sunne beame by day was to
be seene. Onely upon the thursday night Sir George
Summers being upon the watch had an apparition
of a little round light, like a faint Starre, trembling,
and *streaming along with a sparkeling blaze, halfe the
height upon the Maine Mast,* and shooting sometimes from Shroud to Shroud, tempting to settle
as it were upon any of the foure Shrouds; and for
three or foure houres together, or rather more, halfe
the night it kept with us; running sometimes along
the *Maine-yard* to the very end and then returning."
And how Sir George Somers and others observed
it "*with much wonder* and carefulnesse; but upon a
sodaine towards the morning watch, they lost the
sight of it, and knew not what way it made. . . . The
superstitious Sea-men make many constructions of
this Sea-fire, . . . the same (it may be) which the
Grecians call Castor and Pollux, of which, *if one
onely appeared without the other, they took it for an
evil signe of great tempest.* The Italians call it (a
sacred Body) Corpo sancto: The Spaniards call it
Saint Elmo. . . . Could it have served us now
miraculously to have taken our height by, *it might
have strucken amazement,* and a reverence in our
devotions according to the due of a miracle. But

it did not light us any whit the more to our knowne way." [1]   This "sacred Body," "an evill signe of great tempest," is the protoplast of Shakespeare's delicate Ariel of Argier.   Strachey, by the way, has mentioned the storms known to him off Algeere a moment or two earlier.   This is the spirit of whom Prospero demands, "Hast thou . . . performed to point the tempest that I bade thee?"   "To every article," replies Ariel:

> I boarded the king's ship; now on the beak,
> Now in the waist, the deck, in every cabin,
> I flamed amazement.   Sometime I'd divide
> And burn in many places.   On the topmast,
> The yards and bowsprit, would I flame distinctly,
> Then meet and join. . . .

The pages of Strachey are turbulent hereabout with thunder, lightning and rain, with "windes and Seas as mad as fury and rage could make them," with the huge Sea that "brake upon poop and quarter," the terror and danger that "ranne through the whole Ship with much fright and amazement, startled and turned the bloud, and took down the braves of the most hardy Marriner of them all." Indeed, of himself, he says: "The Lord knoweth, I had as little hope as desire of life in the storme, and in this it went beyond my will; because beyond my reason, why we should labour to preserve life. Yet we did, . . . the most despairefull things

[1] Strachey, II, 12.

amongst men being matters of no moment with Him who is the . . . essence of all mercy." Of these conditions there may be some reminiscence in what follows of Shakespeare's account: "The fire and cracks," says Ariel—

> The fire and cracks
> Of sulphurous roaring the most mighty Neptune
> Seem to besiege, and make his bold waves tremble,
> Yea, his dread trident shake.

"My brave spirit," exclaims Prospero—

> Who was so firm, so constant, that this coil
> Would not infect his reason?
> *Ariel*   Not a soul
> But felt a fever of the mad, and play'd
> Some tricks of desperation.

After the wreck upon Prospero's isle—though that be land of faerie in Shakespearian seas far from "the still-vex'd Bermoothes" whence Ariel fetched his dew—the identity of particulars between The Tempest and Strachey's letter persists. Not in Jourdan's narrative, or any other, of Gates's expedition do we find basis for parallels, verbal or incidental, such as the following. Any one might be fortuitous; but taken in the lump, they are impressive: Strachey's search for "running Springs of fresh water," [1]—and Caliban's "fresh springs" and "brine

[1] The quotations from Strachey in this paragraph will be found respectively and in order on pp. 20, 18, 22, 23, 24, 16, 7, 12, 34-35.

pits;" Strachey's "Berries, whereof our men seeth-
ing . . . made a kind of pleasant drink,"—and
Caliban's "water with berries in it;" Strachey's
"Owles and Bats in great store" and a "kinde of
webbe-footed Fowle, . . . which Birds, with, a light
bough in a darke night (as in our Lowbelling) were
caught . . . which for their blindenesse were called
the Sea Owle,"—and Sebastian's suggestion that
they "go a bat-fowling (or lowbelling);" Strachey's
further description of these birds "of the bignesse
of an English greene Plover, or Sea-Meawe [or sea-
mell]," that "breed in those Ilands which are high,
and far alone" and are caught on "the Rockes or
Sands,"—and Caliban's "I'll get thee young sea-
mells [misprinted in the folio, "scamels"] from the
rock;" Strachey's description of the "*Tortoise* . . .
such a kind of meat, as a man can neither absolutely
call *Fish nor Flesh*, keeping most what in the water,
and feeding upon Sea-grasse like a *Heifer*,"—and
Shakespeare's invention of Caliban, who is for Prospero "tortoise," for Trinculo, "Man or a fish? A
strange fish!", for Stephano "moon-calf" on all
occasions.

If the reader is hospitable to further coincidences,
let him note the following: Strachey's "mightiest
blast of lightning and most terrible rap of thunder
that ever astonied mortal man . . . and many
scattering showers of rain which would passe swiftly
over, and yet fall with such force and darknesse for
the time as if it would never bee cleere againe,"

and his earlier, "It could not be said to raine, the waters like whole Rivers did flood in the ayre." Compare Trinculo's discomfort in the frequency and plethora of the storms: "Another storm brewing; yond same black cloud . . . looks like a foul bombard that would shed his liquor. If it should thunder as it did before, I know not where to hide my head: yond same cloud cannot choose but fall by pailfuls. [Thunder] Alas, the storm is come again!"—Earlier, Strachey has told us, "We threw overboard much luggage and staved many a Butte of Beere, Hogsheads of Oyle, Syder, Wine . . . and heaved away all our Ordinance on the starboord side." Compare Shakespeare's Stephano: "I escaped with a butt of sack, which the sailors heaved overboard," and (to Caliban), "Bear this away where my hogshead of wine is."—Strachey's malcontents in Bermuda who arranged to meet our men "at a pond of fresh water;" then "like Outlawes betooke them to the wild woods," "desiring for ever to inhabite heere"; then audaciously demanded of Sir Thomas Gates that he "furnish each of them with two Sutes of Apparell." Compare Shakespeare's Stephano and his viceroys conspiring "to make this island" their "own for ever," who battle their way through woods of toothed briars and thorns and the pond by no means fresh to settle accounts with the master of the isle; arrive at his cell; encounter the suits of "glistering apparel" which he has hung out, and stay their "bloody

thoughts" to make themselves first masters thereof.
This "apparel" motive is neither unique in fiction
nor highly inventive, but it is of a piece with the
fact as recorded in the letter of which Shakespeare
has already made free use. Otherwise it would not
be worth mentioning.

The name Caliban, as everybody has heard, appears to be shaped from Caniba, or Calibana, the
Italian for the land of the Caribbean Indians, supposed to be eaters of men. The name Gonzalo.
also unique in English dramatic literature of the
time, is common in records of travel. In Hakluyt's
Navigations, which undoubtedly Shakespeare had
perused, there are Gonzaluses and Ferdinandos and
Stephanos and other names used in The Tempest.
Such names, as well as Caliban's "Setebos," are
found also in Eden's Historie of Travayle, 1577.
"Prospero", "Ferdinando", "Alonzo", and "Antonio" occur in Thomas's Historye of Italye, 1561;
and "Prospero" and "Stephano", among the
dramatis personæ of the 1601 quarto of Every Man
in his Humor. But the names Gonzalo, and Ferdi-
nand, leap to the eye in Strachey's account of the
shipwreck: "Gonzalus Ferdinandus Oviedus" [1] is
Strachey's authority for the reputation of the "Iland
Bermudas" and its Devils, and he takes pains to
tell her Ladyship, his correspondent, so. Gonzalo
and Ferdinando were already named for Shakespeare
before he set them ashore.

[1] Strachey, 14.

'ouching Stephano, I blush to say that as it is ne who on Prospero's island comes in singing:

> I shall no more to sea, to sea,
> Here shall I die ashore,—

as it is he to whom, ringleader of the baser sort, occurs the thought: "the King and all our company else being drowned, we will inherit here"—as it is Stephano who would be "king o' the isle" with Trinculo and Caliban as viceroys, and who warns Trinculo: "if you prove a mutineer, the next tree;" so in Bermuda it was a Stephen who headed the first dangerous mutiny. Strachey has already told how "the major part of the common sort" were willing "to settle a foundation of *ever inhabiting there*," how secret discontents beginning "in the Seamen . . . had like to have been the parents of bloudy issues and mischiefes," how the seamen joined landsmen to them, and how this first conspiracy was crushed. Now he proceeds: "Yet could not this be any warning to others, who more subtilly began to shake the foundation of our quiet safety, and therein did one Stephen Hopkins commence the first act or overture: A fellow who had much knowledge in the Scriptures, and could reason well therein, whom our minister therefore chose to be his Clarke, to read the Psalmes, and Chapters upon Sondayes." This same Stephen in January "brake" with two others "and alleaged substantiall arguments, both civill and divine (the Scripture

falsly quoted) *that it was no breach of honesty,* conscience, nor Religion, *to decline from the obedience of
the Governour, or refuse to goe any further, led by his
authoritie* (except it so pleased themselves) *since
the authoritie ceased when the wracke was committed,
and with it they were all freed from the government of
any man;* and for a matter of Conscience" they were
"bound each one to provide for himself," and "to
stay in this place," there being "abundance of God's
providence of all manner of goode foode," etc. This
Stephano of real life, brought forth in manacles and
faced by the two accusers with whom he had conversed, made "answere, which was onely full of
sorrow and teares, pleading simplicity and deniall.
But hee being . . . generally held worthy to satis-
fie the punishment of his offence, with the sacrifice
of his life, our Governour passed the sentence of a
Martiall Court upon him, such as belongs to Mutinie
and Rebellion. But so penitent hee was, and made
so much moane, alleadging the ruine of his wife and
children in this his trespasse, as it wrought in the
hearts of all the better sort of the company, who
therefore [Captain Newport and Strachey among
the rest] went unto our Governor . . . and never
left him untill we had got his pardon." [1] Whether
this puritan proponent of freedom from authority
and of "inheriting here" was the contributory evo-
cation of Shakespeare's "drunken butler, Stephano,"
I dare not say. Shakespeare had an ever ready

[1] Strachey, 28, 30–31.

ridicule for the anarch, and a tolerant smile for the extravagances of the Puritan. Stephen was both anarch and sectary; Stephano but the former, and by no means knowledged in the scriptures. It may engage descendants of the Mayflower to know that having returned to England, the Brownist Hopkins, with his second wife and two children of his first, joined himself in 1620 to the Bradford and Brewster expedition and, in more congenial company this time, settled permanently in the Plymouth Colony. As one of the twenty-two passengers on that immemorial craft from whom descent in America has been proved, he has, of his progeny alone, commemorators today more numerous by far than were the colonists whose hearts he softened that day toward the end of January, 1610. This, however, is *desipere in* [or *ex*] *loco*. Whether Shakespeare borrowed names from Strachey or not, to make an argument out of it would be precious and inconsequential. We have already sufficient evidence that he knew his Strachey from first page to last.

If the coincidences between The Tempest and Strachey's letter were confined to details of romantic adventure Shakespeare's interest would not appear to be out of the common. His acquaintance with the document would be proved, but we should have no indication of his political opinion. Does he, like the hungry generation of contemporary dramatists seize upon the plum-duff and forget the rum and blue fire? The sequence may provide the answer.

No sooner has Strachey recounted the safe arrival
of Sir Thomas Gates in Virginia than he proceeds
to describe the disordered state of the Colony [1]—
"not excusing likewise the form of government of
some errour, which was not powerfull among so
headie a multitude—the miserable effects in sloath,
riot and vanity; . . . continual wasting, no hus-
bandry, the old store still spent on, . . . And with
this Idlenesse . . . the headlesse multitude (some
neither of qualitie nor Religion) not imployed to
the end for which they were sent hither; no, not
compelled (since in themselves unwilling) to sowe
corne for their owne bellies, nor to put a Roote,
Herbe, etc. for their owne particular good in their
Gardens or Elsewhere." . . . And this in "one
of the goodliest Countries under the sunne"; for
"no Country yeeldeth goodlier Corne, nor more
manifold increase . . . thousands of goodly Vines
in every hedge and Boske, running along the ground
which yeelde a plentiful Grape in their kinde,"
abundance of all things richly bestowed by nature,
if but manured and dressed by the hand of hus-
bandry, all "suffered to lie sicke and languishe.
Only let me truely acknowledge, they are not an
hundred or two of deboist hands . . . ill provided
for before they came, and worse to be governed when
they are here . . . that must be the carpenters and
workemen in this so glorious a building." With
the usual result in abuse where no provision for

[1] Strachey, 46–51.

legitimate profit had been made, there was no sys-
tematized truck with the Indians. "And for this
misgovernment, chiefly our Colony is much bound
to the Mariners" who dishonestly forestall the
market with them by night; and to the usury of the
Masters, and the frauds of the Pursers. The natural
outcome of communism and divided rule, to be
cured only by "the better authoritie and government now changed into an absolute command."

Something of this "tempest of dissention" had
already been conceded in the True and Sincere
Declaration of December, 1609. And still more had
been embodied from Strachey's Letter to an Excellent Lady in the True Declaration, which as we
know had been published in November, 1610:—
the "Every man overvaluing his owne worth, would
be a Commander; every man underprizing another's
value denied to be commanded;" the "Every man
sharked for his owne booty, but was altogether
carelesse of succeeding penurie;" the "idlenesse,"
the "treasons," the "want of government." But
the account of natural abundance, the corn and
vines and chance for tilth and profit, and of the
wasteful sloth, the "headless multitude" and "privie
faction" of Virginia, in the unpublished letter is
more minute and vivid; and if Shakespeare has so
far been drawing upon the materials of the letter,
it is but natural that he should continue to do so.
It is also natural that as his enchanted island is a
composite of Bermuda and of islands "by wandering

sailors never seen," so also his animadversions upon colonial communism should be a transmutation— neither of Bermudan fact nor of Virginian alone, but of both.

The shafts of Strachey's reality, Shakespeare points with irony. No sooner has the poet brought to shore the shipwrecked king and court of Naples than, out of a clear sky, his wise and loyal Gonzalo with a sort of "merry fooling" animadverts upon the Virginia plantation, and propounds Utopia. "Had I *plantation* of this isle, my lord. . . . And were the king on't, what would I do?" Then, adapting Montaigne's embellishment of the golden age:

> I' the commonwealth I would by contraries
> Execute all things: for no kind of profit
> Would I admit; no name of magistrate;
> Letters should not be known; riches, poverty,
> And use of service, none; contract, succession,
> Bourn, bound of land, tilth, vineyard, none;
> No use of metal, corn, or wine, or oil;
> No occupation; all men idle, all,
> And women too, but innocent and pure;
> No sovereignty.

Upon which the rascally Sebastian, "Yet he would be king on't;" and Antonio, "The latter end of his commonwealth forgets the beginning." But Gonzalo, still playing with Montaigne and communism— may we not say in the light of the Virginian fiasco?—

All things in common Nature should produce
Without sweat or endeavour; treason, felony,
Sword, pike, knife, gun, or need of any engine
Would I not have; but Nature should bring forth,
Of its own kind, all foison,—all abundance,
To feed my innocent people.

These, "all idle" and "knaves," Gonzalo "would with such perfection govern, Sir, T' excel the golden age." So the subacid Gonzalo, of the kingless commonwealth of which he should be king. So with exemplification by contraries, Shakespeare in the sequel of his play—the speedy treasons of Sebastian and Antonio "where no name of magistrate is known," the inheriting ambitions and "bloody thoughts" of the "deboshed" and idle poor. And so, Strachey and Sandys drawing upon him, of the plantation where "every man would be a Commander."

The improvidence resulting from the original common stock system in the plantation of Virginia, and the anarchy where none was "sole and absolute governor," were precisely the curses which, when Shakespeare's whimsical "plantation of this isle" was put upon the stage, the friends of Shakespeare in the Virginia Council were striving to lift from the shoulders of their colony.

III

In this exposition of the relation of The Tempest
to its colonial origin, the purpose has been not so
much to show that Shakespeare was alive to a matter
of contemporary interest and had his definite opinion
concerning the political questions involved—so had
every alert Englishman of the day,—as to show
that, aside from hearsay, his main source of information was a letter so revelatory, so confidential, that
it could not be, and was not, published at the time.
That he should have had access to a manuscript
privately circulated among members of the Virginia Council, Southampton, Sandys, and the rest,
is of significance, more vital than has hitherto been
recognized, in our understanding of Shakespeare's
intimacy with the leaders of the Virginia enterprise;
and that it has not been generally recognized is due
largely to the fact that until recently historians and
editors, not considering that intimacy and its possi-
bilities, have loosely conveyed the idea that the
poet's source of information was published between
1610 and 1612. This they have accomplished by
manifold devices: by coupling it, as a narrative accessible to all, with tracts or pamphlets actually
published during that period; or by citing it with
such tracts under the title, A True Reportory, which
was not coined by Strachey, nor known to anyone
till the publication of the letter by Purchas in 1625;
or by speaking of it under that title as "reprinted

in 1625," thus implying an earlier publication; or by christening it "a publication, possibly printed in 1612," or, with definite and unpardonable inexactitude, "a tract which appeared in 1610–12;" or, still worse, by gratuitously apprising us that "this pamphlet was written in 1610, and printed in London before the close of the same year"—a statement calculated to deceive the very elect. Of recent scholars, I am glad to note that Professor Greene in his edition of The Tempest says that Shakespeare "may have seen the original manuscript, perhaps while it was in the keeping of Hakluyt, who transmitted it to Purchas;" [1] and that Mr. Morton Luce holds that "he must surely have seen it." [2] What some have conjectured, I hope has been proved here once and for all.

It may be well to recapitulate the history of Strachey's letter, so far as known. It was, as we have seen, addressed to an Excellent Lady in England. It was brought to a close at Algernoone Fort, Point Comfort, July 15, 1610. It was forwarded the same day by Sir Thomas Gates, who arrived in England in September of that year. Who the lady was may possibly yet be determined; but since we are not here indulging in conjecture, I have relegated my own guess to a less conspicuous corner. [3] At the

[1] H. E. Greene, The Tempest, p. viii, in The Tudor Shakespeare, 1913.

[2] Morton Luce, The Tempest, pp. 149–161, in The Arden Shakespeare.

[3] See below, Appendix C.

time of Hakluyt's death, 1616, the manuscript passed
with other of his papers into the hands of Samuel
Purchas, by whom it was included, under the title,
A True Reportory, etc., in Purchas his Pilgrimes,
issued from the press in 1625. Neither the British
Museum nor the Bodleian Library owns, or knows,
of any edition printed before that date. No other
library, European or American, has ever announced
possession of an earlier edition or knowledge of its
existence. Nor has any book collector. No record
of printed books—the Register of the Stationers'
Company, or subsidiary record—has ever listed a
printed copy other than that of Purchas. No scholar,
however nodding, has dreamed, or dreamed of telling us, that he has seen a copy printed before 1625.
As to the original manuscript, the Keeper of manuscripts in the British Museum writes, in answer to
my query, "I have made a complete search under
Strachey's name, and under Bermudas, Somers'
Islands, Summer Islands, without success. We have
nothing of William Strachey except the travels
through Virginia in Sloane MS. 1622." My correspondent, Miss Parker, at the Bodleian Library reports, "I have made an exhaustive search for MS.
of A True Reportory of the Wracke, etc., but have
met with no success. The Bodleian certainly contains no such MS. Everything seems to point to
the fact that the 'Reportory' was not printed until
Purchas got hold of it; and it seems highly probable
that the Ms. has perished."

Considering all the premises it is, moreover, "practically inconceivable that the original manuscript of Strachey's narrative, or an early copy of it, can be on record as existing without having been promptly published by some student of Shakespeare." So writes my friend, Mr. A. W. Pollard, Assistant Keeper of printed books in the British Museum, in an informal response to my inquiries. He continues: "For the same reason it is inconceivable that a printed edition earlier than that of 1625 can be on record. Furthermore (and this is less obvious) it is practically inconceivable that the Reportory should have got into print in 1610-12, and all copies of it disappeared." This is true for its contents would have created a tremendous sensation and would have been exploited by the Court party as damaging to the control of the Liberals in the Virginia enterprise. "It would have ruined Strachey's career," proceeds Mr. Pollard, "to have published it at such a time; the Wardens of the Stationers' Company would never have passed it, and it could only have been printed secretly, and about this time to the best of my belief no secret printing was going on." This is significant. So far as the present writer knows, the only publication dealing with political affairs in Virginia that appeared during these years, without license of the Stationers' Company (which itself, was a member of the Virginia Company), got itself into print—not secretly but by indirection—under the patronage of clergymen who were disaffected with the policy of the Virginia Council. That publication is a eulogy of the deposed and discontented Captain John Smith: an adverse criticism of the management of the enterprise under the Patriot party in the Council. It is entitled The Proceedings of the English Colonie in Virginia . . . 1606–1612, was compiled probably by the Reverend William Symonds, and was printed in the latter year, not in London but at Oxford, by one Joseph Barnes. The Register of the Stationers' Hall shows, continues Mr. Pollard, that during these critical years, "books about the Virginia Company's affairs were entered 'under the hands' of very influential persons, as a guarantee of their being harmless. The company was getting up two lotteries, and doing its best to repair the fiasco of 1609–10. Now, Strachey's account is written of course as by a well-wisher of the company to another well-wisher, but to my thinking it is much too frank to have been allowed in print while a very influential company was trying to raise more men and more money. Hence its circulation in manuscript, in which form Shakespeare may, of course, have read it, if he didn't, as Kipling plausibly contends, get his knowledge from a drunken seaman."

Mr. Kipling's contention, as we have observed, cannot dispose of the numerous and frequently unique resemblances between The Tempest and Strachey's narrative. And the inconceivability of that narrative having found its way into print before

The Tempest was written corroborates the conclusion from historical evidence at which I had already arrived. The letter was not printed so long as the Virginia Company was in the control of the Patriot party. It was printed one year after the Patriots were suppressed and the Virginia charters annulled; and then, 1625, by an editor recognized as the official historian of James and the tyrannical party at Court.

Though Strachey returned to England late in October, or early in November, 1611, and was lodging the next year in Blackfriars, information derived personally from him could not permeate a play acted on the first of November, 1611. And even if one cling to the indefensible supposition that The Tempest was not acted before February, 1613, the close verbal and literary coincidences between the play and the letter are of such a kind as could not be accounted for by any mere conversation that Shakespeare may have had with Strachey.

Sir Thomas Gates, who brought to England the Letter to an Excellent Lady, was a member of the council. The letter was entrusted by this lady to influential members of the council, and one of them, probably Sir Edwin Sandys, incorporated from it such portions as were fitting for the True Declaration issued to the public; and Hakluyt was allowed to file it away for printing in a supplement to his Discoveries of the World when the right time should come. Sir Thomas Gates and Richard Hakluyt were of the four original adventurers nominated as principals in the earliest charter of the London Company, 1606, and were vitally concerned in the success of the colony. The letter was always in the keeping of those vitally concerned until Purchas got hold of it. That Shakespeare was allowed to read it and to use certain of its materials for a play, as with just discrimination and due discretion he did, is illustrative of the closeness of his intimacy with the patriot leaders of the Virginia enterprise.

IV

Among the poets of Shakespeare's circle a few had been celebrating "fruitfullest Virginia" from the day of Spenser down. Samuel Daniel had sung of Virginia in his Musophilus of 1603:

And who in time, knows whither we may vent
The treasure of our tongue? To what strange shores
This gain of our best glory shall be sent;
T'enrich unknowing nations with our stores?
What worlds in th' yet unforméd Occident
May come refin'd with accents that are ours,
Or who can tell for what great work in hand
The greatness of our style is now ordain'd?

He dedicated the poem to that patron of the Virginian adventure, Fulke Greville, of whose proximity to Shakespeare in Stratford we are aware. At various points the career of Daniel touches that of Shakespeare. He was a protégé and praiser of Southampton, and a tutor in the Pembroke family; and in this same year, 1603, we find his name associated with those of Shakespeare, Holland, Jonson, Drayton, Chapman, Marston, as among the "most pregnant witts of these our times" still living.

In 1605, Ben Jonson, collaborating in a comedy of frequent reference to Virginia, got into trouble for a passage written by his colleague, Marston, in which it is suggested that, if the King's brother Scots would only betake themselves to the new plantation, "wee shoulde finde ten times more comfort of them there then wee doe heere." Said Jonson to Drummond of Hawthornden: "He was delated by Sir James Murray to the King, for writting something against the Scots, in a play Eastward Hoe, and voluntarily imprissonned himself with Chapman and Marston, who had written it [the play] amongst them. The report was that they should then [have] had their ears cut and noses. After their delivery, he banqueted all his friends; there was Camden, Selden and others; at the midst of the feast his old Mother drank to him" and showed him poison which she would have mixed in his drink, "if the sentence had taken execution." Henceforward, Jonson rather religiously refrained from references to Virginia. But he could not keep his hands off altogether. In his Staple of Newes (1625) he pokes fun at "the blessed Pokahontas, the great king's daughter of Virginia," for "coming forth of," therefore having entered into "the womb of a Tavern."

In 1606, Shakespeare's friend Drayton crowned himself laureate of the new English world. His Ode to the Virginia Voyage has the proper pith and swing:

> You brave heroique minds,
> Worthie your countries name,
>   That honour still pursue,
>   Goe and Subdue,
> Whilst loytering hinds
> Lurk here at home with shame! . . .
>
> And in regions farre,
> Such heroes bring yee foorth
>   As those from whom we came;
>   And plant our name
> Under that starre
> Not knowne unto our north!

Still another of Shakespeare's fellows touches upon colonial events, George Chapman, who in his Epicede on Prince Henry, 1612, describes the tempest off the Bermudas already immortalized by the greater poet: a lumbering effort. To Chapman's Masque of the Two Inns of Court, 1613, with its troop of Virginia priests and princes doing homage at the nuptials of the Palgrave and the Princess Elizabeth, I have already referred.

There are other mentions of Virginia in the literary prose and verse of the day; but on the whole the use made by the poets of this chapter of contemporary history is slight and of little imaginative worth. When we consider the failure of others to realize the momentous implications, our feeling is not so much of wonder that Shakespeare made little use of destinies still on the knees of the Gods, as of happy recognition that, when he made drama of the environing romance, he failed not to make also shrewd allusion to the political breakers, the tempest of dissension that nearly drove the venture on the rocks. If to him and not to his colleague, Fletcher, could with certainty be assigned the eulogy to James I written about 1612 for the last scene of Henry VIII:

Wherever the bright sun of heaven shall shine,
His honour and the greatness of his name
Shall be and make new nations. He shall flourish,
And, like a mountain cedar, reach his branches
To all the plains about him. Our children's children
Shall see this and bless Heaven—

we might rejoice that, so far as "our children's children" are concerned, what were perhaps his latest lines were those of "a prophet new inspired." But Shakespeare did not write them. They are in the cadence and diction of Fletcher.[1] Still the prophecy

[1] The rhythms of the scene are in general those of Fletcher. The diction and figure of the lines quoted above are a reminiscence of Beaumont and Fletcher's Philaster (1610) V, v. 213-215: "That you may grow yourselves over all lands. And live to see your plenteous branches spring Wherever there is sun"

lives in their joint name; and, little as the future
conduct of James justified any encomium, the lines
will breathe to all time the confidence of one of
Shakespeare's friends in the blessing that England
was to confer upon the world: for the plantation of
England in Virginia was a Christian crusade as well
as a commercial and political undertaking.

(by Beaumont); and of V, iii, 26–30, "These two fair cedar-
branches, the noblest of the mountain where they grew straight-
est and tallest, under whose still shades," etc. (by Fletcher).
The figure of tree and shade, of course biblical, occurs also
in the Virginia Council's True and Sincere Declaration of Dec. 4,
1609.

CHAPTER IV

THE LEADER OF THE LIBERAL MOVEMENT—SIR EDWIN SANDYS

VERY close to Southampton, Pembroke, Sackville, Neville, Gates, Brooke, Selden, Digges and the Ferrars in the effort, between 1608 and 1624, to erect a free state in Virginia, stood Sir Edwin Sandys, the son of the Archbishop of York. Whether Sandys and Shakespeare were personally acquainted we know not, but they had friends in common; and that they sympathized with the political ideals of the same master, we shall soon have abundant proof. A man "of rare gifts and knowledge and great resoluteness, the incomparable leader of the liberal statesmen, one of the greatest men of a great age," Sir Edwin was the noblest patriot of the first quarter of the seventeenth century. From 1607 to 1624 he was a member of the Virginia Council, and in that council was always an ardent advocate of reform. It was he who drafted the charter of 1609 by which certain evils of the Virginia government were removed. And it was, in all probability, he who prepared the instructions given to Gates in that year, as "sole and absolute governor," for the suppression of factions and mutinies by martial law

and the institution of civil order. "In all matters
of Civil Jùstice," says the author, "you shall find
it properest and usefullest to proceed rather upon
the naturall right and equitie than upon the nice-
ness and lettre of the lawe." [1]   In the preparation
and confirmation of the improved charter of 1612,
Sandys was prominent. He favored and supported
the institution of free tenancy and the development
of private holdings, by which Governor Dale in
1614 prepared the colony for its transition from the
communistic and plantation type to that of individual effort and provincial economy. In 1617
Sandys became assistant-treasurer of the council,
and from that date his ascendancy is marked. To
his effort was largely due the charter of 1618, by
which provision was made for the establishment of
representative government in Virginia; and it was
under his treasurership, or governorship, of the company in 1619 that the first Virginia Assembly con-
vened—"the first example of a domestic parliament
to regulate the internal concerns of this country,
which was afterwards cherished throughout America
as the dearest birthright of freemen." [2]

In Parliament, Sandys was of the popular party
in opposition from 1604 to 1614. From the first,
we find him insisting that the general and perpetual
voice of men is as the voice of God himself. In

[1] Ashmolean MS., quoted by H. L. Osgood, Am. Col. Seventeenth Century, I, 63.
[2] Brown, Eng. Pol. in Va., and authorities as cited, p. 29.

committee in the House of Commons, 1606, he says, "When written law is wanting, we must fall back upon precedent; when precedent fails, upon the *ratio naturalis*," that is to say, collective reason, the common sense of mankind.[1] This was the interpretation of the law of nature and of nature's God recently enunciated by Sandys's great teacher, Richard Hooker, in the treatise Of the Laws of Ecclesiastical Polity,—an interpretation not unfamiliar to Shakespeare. In 1612 Sandys is a leader in the Remonstrance against the King's conduct toward Parliament. In 1614 his famous speech of May 21 sounds the keynote of the constitutional reform which he helped to achieve in both America and England. He maintained that even though a Parliament would, it "cannot give liberty to the king to make laws;" that "the origin of every monarchy lay in election;" that this election was two fold, "of person and of care"—in other words, "not only of the individual entrusted with executive authority but of the character and limitations of that authority;" that "the people gave its consent to the king's authority upon the express understanding that there were certain reciprocal conditions which neither king nor people might violate with immunity; and that a king who pretended to rule by any other title, such as that of conquest, might be dethroned, whenever there was force sufficient to overthrow

[1] Nathan Abbott, Characteristics of the Common Law, St. Louis Congress of Arts and Science, II, 279.

him." [1]   Here again the idea was derived from
Richard Hooker.   The political concepts involved,
as we shall presently see, are those of Shakespeare's
Richard II (1595–7), and of the later plays in so
far as reference is made to the relation of ruler and
subject.   For the six years following 1614 there
were no parliaments.   From 1621 till after the death
of James, Sandys heads the patriots in the House
of Commons—always the proponent and defender
of free institutions and free speech.

Of Hooker, Sandys had been the pupil at Corpus
Christi, Oxford, and he remained his lifelong friend.
Like Hooker, he was a firm supporter of the discipline
of the Church of England, and in his youth, at any
rate, an active opponent of the separatist tendencies
of Brownists and Barrowists.   Like his master he
favored, however, the emancipation of the mind in
matters of religious belief; and in his maturer years
he became, as we shall see, the champion of the
Separatists themselves in their efforts to secure
freedom as regarding forms of worship and ecclesiastical regimen in the New World.   Civil liberty
he had advocated from his youth, but, again like
his master, in terms of obedience to constitutional
order and to a law higher still—the unchanging
expression of universal reason.   Hooker admired
the polity of Calvin's Republic of Geneva, but
distrusted the dogmatism of scriptural infallibility

[1] D'Ewes's Journals of the House of Commons, I, 492–3;
and a paraphrase in D. N. B., art. Edwin Sandys.

upon which that theocracy rested. Sandys, "at harte opposed to the government of a monarchie," went beyond his master in admiration of the Genevan Republic; but largely because the civil polity of Geneva appeared to furnish a model, neither autocratic nor purely democratic, but of the aristo-democratic mean. To Hooker's teaching, to the political wisdom of Sandys, to the legal experience of such men as Selden and Brooke,[1] to the practical intrepidity of these and of Southampton, Sir Edward Sackville, the Ferrars, and their fellow-patriots in the Virginia Company and in Parliament, America owes the colonial charters of 1609, 1612, 1618 with their successive triumphs over royal prerogative; and to them it owes the institution of commonwealths where the idea of English liberalism was to attain fruition. To them we owe the idea of a state whose sovereignty is in all the people, but whose government, in the hands of their chosen representatives ruling by law of public approbation— the idea of an ordered economy of equal rights, but of function according to degree of merit and ability.

The solicitude displayed by Sandys in matters of civil polity is manifest as early as 1609, also in regard to matters of religious liberty. No sooner had the charter of that year been wrested from the king than invitation was sent to "His Majesty's

[1] For Sir Francis Bacon, in politics a reactionary and absolutist, but associated with Selden, Brooke, and Sandys in the preparation of Letters Patent for Virginia, see Appendix D.

subjects in the Free States of the United Provinces, offering them in an English colony in America the place of refuge which they were seeking in the Netherlands." [1]   At that time, because of the opposition of the Archbishop of Canterbury and the king, the move came to nothing.   But of "His Majesty's subjects" those most concerned, even then, were the future Pilgrims to New England; and in the invitation the hand of Sandys is unmistakable. His interest in at least one of the leaders of the English Separatists in Holland, William Brewster, was personal and of long standing.   In their youth they must have frequently met in the little village of Scrooby, which was the home of Brewster; while the Manor House close by was the property of Edwin's older brother, Sir Samuel Sandys, and was at various times inhabited by Edwin himself.   They had, as mutual friend, George Cranmer, who was beloved of Sandys from boyhood and was Brewster's colleague in the official household of Queen Elizabeth's Secretary of State, Davison.   In 1585 we find Cranmer and Brewster accompanying the Secretary as assistants, on an embassy to Holland.   Cranmer and Sandys were at the time fresh from the tuition of Richard Hooker, and thrilling with his idealism, humanism, prophetic inspiration.   A few years later they are counseling their tutor in the preparation of his Ecclesiastical Polity.

[1] Brown, Eng. Pol. in Va., p. 15.

In 1600 Cranmer "a gentleman of singular hopes" died. But the connection between Sandys and Brewster continued. The latter had returned to Scrooby in 1588. Till his departure for Holland in 1608 he was living there, and as late as 1607 was conducting the prayer meetings of the Separatists in the Manor House of Sir Samuel Sandys, "a firm advocate of toleration."

In 1608, Brewster and the Reverend John Robinson with their Separatist congregation made their escape from Scrooby and the surrounding villages to Holland. The proposed emigration to America of the next year was, as we have seen, for the time abandoned; but in 1617 two of their congregation, then of Leyden, visited London and "found the Virginia Company very desirous to have them go" to America, "and willing to grant them a patent with as ample privileges as they had or could grant to any." In order to remove the objections of the king and others to the religious purposes of the Separatists, a letter of seven articles, signed by Robinson and Brewster, was conveyed to the Virginia Council. In response to this we find Sandys, then assistant-treasurer, sending on November 12 his "hartie salutations" to Robinson and Brewster and assuring them not only that the articles are acceptable, but that the agents of the congregation in London have "carried themselves with good discretion." His letter concludes: "If therefore it may please God so to directe your desires as that in your parts there fall out no just impediments, I trust by the same direction it shall likewise appear that, on our parte, all forwardness to set you forward shall be found in the best note which with reason may be expected. And so I betake you with this designe (which I hope verily is the worke of God) to the gracious protection and blessing of the Highest." He subscribes himself "Your very loving friend." [1]   When, in 1620, the Pilgrims set sail, it was with a promise obtained by Sandys from the king that their freedom to worship as they pleased, though not formally ratified by royal authority, should at any rate be connived at; and the grant with which they set sail—that of February, 1620— had been "examined and sealed in view of and with approbation of the members [of the council] present" at the house of Sir Edwin Sandys, then governor of the company, near Aldersgate. It confirmed the Pilgrims in all the privileges of a body politic already assured by charter to the colonists of Southern Virginia: freedom of person, equality before the law, the right to participate in the government of themselves, and to enjoy all liberties, franchises, and immunities as if they had been abiding and born within the realm of England. "For the present," says their pastor, the Rev. John Robinson, in his farewell letter to the whole ship's company, "you are to have only them for your ordinarie

---

[1] Bradford, Plymouth Plantation, p. 31; and E. D. Neill, History of the Virginia Company of London, 122–129.

Governours, which your selves shall make choyse of for that worke."

Such had been the service rendered by Sandys to the founders of New England. There can be no doubt that the qualities displayed by William Brewster, as Elder of the congregation in Leyden and afterwards in the Plymouth Colony were colored by long association with his "very loving friend," Sir Edwin Sandys and their intimate from youth, George Cranmer, as well as by a first-hand acquaintance with the printed word of Richard Hooker. This kinship with the school of that great master is reflected in the genial humanity, the liberal knowledge and outlook, the conservative wisdom, with which the historic Elder moulded the civil polity of the first settlement in New England, and held in check tendencies elsewhere manifested toward religious bigotry and oppression.

Time and again Sandys resisted the king's arbitrary dictation in the Virginia Company. His election to the governorship for a second term, in 1620, the king forbade,—"declaring that he was his greatest enemy, and that he could hardly think well of whomsoever was his friend," and concluding, "Choose the Devil if you will but not Sir Edwin Sandys". Southampton, whom the patriots thereupon elected instead, undertook the office, saying, "I know the king will be angry at it, but so the expectation of this pious and glorious work may be encouraged, let the company do with me what they please." For their determination to found in America the free state which they could not found at home, Sandys and Southampton, Selden, Lord Cavendish, and the Ferrars, more than once, suffered arrest and confinement at the king's pleasure. More than once these men, and friends of men, with whom Shakespeare spake, were charged with nefarious political designs against the king's prerogative within the realm of Britain itself. The king was warned by the Spanish ambassador that "though they might have a fair pretence for their meetings, yet his majesty would find in the end that the Virginia Court in London would prove a seminary for a seditious parliament." Count Gondomar told truth. Selden, Sandys, Nicholas Ferrar, Jr., Sir Dudley Digges, Hoskins and Martin, Neville, Brooke, Phillips, and others interested in the company represented the party of reform in Parliament. Southampton represented it in the Privy Council. It was Digges (the brother of Shakespeare's Leonard) who, with Eliot and Pym, impeached the Duke of Buckingham before the bar of the House of Lords in 1626. It was Selden (the friend of Shakespeare's Brooke) who instigated the memorable Protest of 1621 on the rights and privileges of the Commons; and in 1628 moved and helped to carry through the House the Petition of Right. In the Virginia Company were the forerunners, nay, the confederates of the Hampdens, Strodes and Cromwells who were to bring the son of James to the scaffold and establish constitutional government in England. In the Virginia Company, these men and their fellow-patriots were already, by the charters of 1609–18, the founders of representative government in Virginia; and by the charter of 1620, of representative government in New England, as well.

But the most indefatigable of the founders was Sir Edwin Sandys. "An almost ideal administrator," as Professor Osgood has called him, it was during his supremacy in the Virginia Council that the seeds were sown of the liberties of America. He supported Gates and Dale in the suppression of faction, fraud, and idleness. He devoted himself to the extinction of communistic proprietorship, to the proper development of the public lands and the encouragement at the same time of private plantations. He strove to keep out the dissolute with whom King James would flood the colony, and to people it instead with self-respecting and industrious farmers and artisans. He set himself to diversify the industries of Virginia, to make provision for the maintenance of religious worship and instruction, and to endow a college for the colony. He prepared the way for an administrative organization and a political system. He was the heart of that group of statesmen, Southampton, Brooke, Selden, Sackville, and the Ferrars, who originated and made effective the "great charter" of 1618, and who thus conferred an equal, uniform, and free government upon the colony.[1] It was

[1] H. L. Osgood, Am. Col., Seventeenth Century, 80–91. Neill,

during his administration that the first representative assembly of Virginia met. No wonder that in the spring of the next year, 1621, the Spanish ambassador should tell James I "it was time for him to look to the Virginia Courts which were kept at the Ferrars' house, where too many of his nobility and gentry resorted to accompany the popular Lord Southampton and the dangerous Sandys." Behind Southampton Sandys was the moving force when, in August of that year, the Virginia Court drew up an ordinance and constitution for the colony, the intent of which was "by the divine assistance to settle in Virginia such a form of government as may be to the greatest benefit and comfort of the people, and whereby all injustice, grievances, and oppression may be prevented and kept off as much as possible from the said colony." And when, soon afterwards, a conspiracy was hatched by the Earl of Warwick, Captain Bargrave, and others of the Court party to annul the free charters, and the king had placed the leaders of the Patriot party under arrest, it was against Sandys that the animus was directed. "By his long acquaintance with Sandys and his wayes," said Bargrave, "he was induced verilie to believe that there was not any man in the world that carried a more malitious heart to the government of a Monarchie, than Sir Edwin Sandys did; that he had moved the Archbishop of Canterbury to give leave to the

Va. Co. of London, 137–8; Brown, First Republic in America, 291.

Brownists and Separatists to go to Virginia, and that Sandys had told him his purpose was to erect a free popular state there, himself and his assured friends to be leaders, and that he was the means of sending the charter into Virginia, in which is a clause that the inhabitants should have no government putt upon them but by their own consente." [1] In spite of what King James did in 1624, with the help of Warwick, Lionel Cranfield, Sir Thomas Smith and the rest of the reactionaries, to rob the colony of its political rights and to destroy all evidence of the liberal purpose and achievement of the Virginia Corporation, the political principles that inspired Sandys, Southampton, Selden, Brooke, Sackville, Cavendish, the Ferrars, and all that noble company, never died out of Virginia, never died out of the northern colony, called New England. These were principles first logically developed and clearly formulated by the tutor of Sir Edwin Sandys, Richard Hooker. Disciples of Hooker, associates of Shakespeare, were the founders of the first republics in the New World.

Sir Edwin was not the only member of the Sandys family interested in Virginia. His older brother, Sir Samuel, a friend and abettor of Elder Brewster, was member of the Council for Virginia in 1612 and stood by Edwin in the company and in Parliament. Their youngest brother, George, joined the company in 1612, was treasurer of the colony in Virginia in 1621 and member of the council there for several

[1] Brown, Eng. Pol. in Va., 37, 41, 47, 209; Genesis, II, 993.

years.   It was in Virginia that he completed his
classic translation of Ovid's Metamorphoses.   The
reader may be interested to learn, moreover, that the
families of Sandys and Washington were connected.
Samuel Sandys, a grandson of Sir Samuel, married
Elizabeth Washington, widow of an ancestral kinsman of George Washington; and another nephew of
Sir Edwin's, Robert Sandys, married Alice Washington of Sulgrave, a great-great-aunt of our first President.   Robert's father, by the way—and this for the
snapper up of unconsidered trifles—was godson and
namesake of Shakespeare's "Justice Shallow." Sir
Thomas Lucy of Charlecote.[1]

[1] For these items and the Sandys genealogy, see Genesis U. S.,
II, 993–995.

CHAPTER V

RICHARD HOOKER, AND THE PRINCIPLES OF AMERICAN LIBERTY

In Sandys and Shakespeare we recognize the religious ideal of freedom tempered by reverence, the political ideal of liberty regulated by law and conserved by delegated authority, the moderation, tolerance of divergent opinion, the broad and sympathetic confidence in progress rather than in rigidity or finality, that are characteristic of the most philosophical writer upon politics, the broadest minded, most learned, and most eloquent divine of sixteenth-century England. That not only Sandys and his co-founders of colonial liberty, but also their successors, the initiators of the American Revolution, owe the central concepts of their political philosophy to Richard Hooker is not difficult to show. That the political concept of Shakespeare's Richard II (1595–1597), and of his later plays in so far as reference is made to the relation of ruler and ruled, is directly influenced by Hooker's Ecclesiastical Polity may be impossible of proof; but that a vivid consimility of thought, not only political, but moral and psychological, obtains, may I think be shown beyond peradventure. In the present chapter we shall consider the influence of Hooker upon the thought of his political contemporaries and their successors in America.

Born in Exeter in 1553, Richard Hooker was of a family by no means without honor in provincial affairs, in law, and in letters. His great-grandfather had been mayor of Exeter, and through several reigns he was member of Parliament. His grandfather, too, had been mayor of that city. His father's brother, John, chamberlain of Exeter, was not only a member of Parliament and of reputation at the bar, but a learned antiquary. Editor-in-chief of the 1586–7 issue of Holinshed's Chronicles, he contributed several augmentations to that monumental work; and of some of these Shakespeare makes use. With pecuniary assistance from this uncle and through his influence with Bishop Jewell, young Hooker was enabled in 1568 to enter Corpus Christi College, Oxford, with a clerkship. By the kindly interest of Jewell he was brought to the knowledge of Bishop Sandys, afterwards Archbishop of York. There resulted the tutorship, beginning in 1573, of the Archbishop's son, Edwin, then twelve or thirteen years of age, and of young Cranmer, grand-nephew of the martyr. "Between Mr. Hooker and these his two pupils, there was a sacred friendship," writes Walton, "a friendship made up of religious principles, which increased daily by a similitude of inclinations to the same recreations and studies; a friendship elemented in youth, and in an university free from self-ends, which the friendships of age usually are not: and in this sweet, this blessed, this spiritual amity, they went on for many years." When they left college Hooker continued with his studies, "still enriching his quiet and capacious soul with the precious learning of the philosophers, casuists, and schoolmen; and with them the foundation and reason of all laws, both sacred and civil." As fellow of his college and lecturer in Logic and in Hebrew he gained wide and honorable recognition. In 1585, upon recommendation of his old patron, Archbishop Sandys, and others, he was appointed Master of the Temple in London. There his views, already pronounced, in opposition to the "discipline" of the Puritans as to public worship, plunged him into controversy with the leaders of the Presbyterian party, and impelled him to the composition of a treatise in justification "of the Laws of Ecclesiastical Polity." For the completion of this treatise he retired in 1591 to the country vicarage of Boscombe; and in 1592 the first four books were entered at Stationers' Hall. They were not published, however, till 1594. The fifth followed in 1597. The remaining three books, published in part from his manuscripts, did not appear till long after the year of his death—1600. The portions of the Polity which especially engage our attention are the Preface (to the reformers of church discipline), the first book, and a few sections of the second. These divisions establish the basis of ecclesiastical laws in "law in general,

both human and divine," outline the political theory
of which the influence is clear in Sandys and the
patriots of the Virginia Council, and enunciate principles, political and philosophical, to which there is a
strikingly remarkable resemblance in various utterances of Shakespeare. No reader or thinker of the
day could, indeed, have escaped the influence of
Hooker. For, though not an innovator, he was a
builder; his treatise "is the first independent work
in English prose of notable power and genius, and
the vigor and grasp of its thoughts are not more
remarkable than the felicity of its literary style." [1]
Said King James, in one of his intervals of illumina-
tion, "Though many others write well, yet in the
next age they will be forgotten; but doubtless there
is in every page of Mr. Hooker's book the picture of a
divine soul, such pictures of Truth and Reason, and
drawn in so sacred colours, that they shall never
fade, but give an immortal memory to the author."
And Pope Clement VIII bears witness: "There is no
learning that this man hath not searched into; nothing too hard for his understanding; this man indeed
deserves the name of an author; his books will get
reverence by age, for there is in them such seeds of
eternity, that if the rest be like this, they shall last
'till the last fire shall consume all learning." [2]

That Sandys's theory of government by popular

[1] T. F. Henderson, Art., Richard Hooker, Encyc. Brit.
[2] Hooker's Works (ed. Keble), I, 71–72, Walton's Life of
Hooker.

consent, and the underlying political philosophy which, through the efforts of the Patriot party in the Virginia Company, became concrete in the earliest representative governments of America, drew their immediate inspiration from Richard Hooker will be apparent to anyone who reads some fifteen pages in sections eight to ten of the first book Of the Laws of Ecclesiastical Polity and half a dozen pages on either side. It will also be apparent that the same concepts underlie the contention and the language of the fathers of American independence. For our present purpose a few excerpts arranged under appropriate headings, with occasional italicizing of lines whose import passed, even though by unconscious process, into the mind of our Revolutionary forefathers and into the Declaration of Independence, will suffice.[1]

1. Equality under the Law of Human Nature or Reason.—"God therefore is a law both to himself," says Hooker, "and to all other things beside. . . . *Who the guide of nature but only the God of nature?* . . . The general and perpetual voice of men is as the sentence of God himself. For that which all men have at all times learned, Nature herself must needs have taught; and God being the author of Nature, her voice is but his instrument.[2] . . . Those things which are equal must needs all have one meas-

[1] The most accessible edition is Ronald Bayne's in Everyman's Library, no. 201. To that the references that follow are made.
[2] Polity, 152, 159, 176.

ure. . . . *From which relation of equality between
ourselves and them that are as ourselves,* what several
rules and canons natural Reason hath drawn for
direction of life no man is ignorant.[1] . . . We see
then how nature itself teacheth laws and statutes
to live by. The laws which have been hitherto
mentioned [of natural Reason] do bind men absolutely even as they are men, although they have
never any settled fellowship, never any solemn
argument amongst themselves what to do or not to
do." [2] And there is "no impossibility in nature
considered by itself, but that men might have lived
without any public regiment." [3] In other words,
the state of nature though not yet political is not
lawless; it is social: the *vox perpetua populi* is the *vox
Dei;* reason and equality prevail, and, save for the
presupposition of corruption, peace might also reign.

2. The ~~Social Compact~~ and the Body Politic.—
"But forasmuch as we are not by ourselves sufficient
to furnish ourselves with competent store of things
needful for such a life as our nature doth desire, a
life fit for the dignity of man; therefore to supply
those defects and imperfections which are in us
living single and solely by ourselves, we are naturally
induced to seek communion and fellowship with
others. *This was the cause of men's uniting themselves at the first in politic Societies, which societies*

---

[1] Polity, 180.
[2] Polity, 188; so also paragraphs 2 and 3, following.
[3] Polity, 191.

could not be without Government, nor Government without a distinct kind of Law from that which hath been already declared. Two foundations there are which bear up public societies: the one, a natural inclination, whereby all men desire sociable life and fellowship, the other, an order expressly or secretly agreed upon touching the manner of their union in living together. *The latter is that which we call the Law of a Commonweal, the very soul of a politic body, the parts whereof are by law animated, held together and set at work in such actions as the common good requireth.*"

3. The Transition to Positive Law; the Pursuit of Happiness.—"Laws politic, ordained for eternal order and regiment amongst men are never framed as they should be, unless presuming the will of man to be inwardly obstinate, rebellious, and averse from all obedience unto *the sacred laws of his nature;* in a word, unless presuming man to be in regard of his depraved mind little better than a wild beast, they do accordingly provide notwithstanding so to frame his outward actions, that they be no hindrance unto the common good for which societies are instituted; unless they do this they are not perfect. . . . All men desire to lead in this world a *happy life. That life is led most happily wherein all virtue is exercised without impediment or let.* . . .

4. Government by Consent of the Governed.— "To take away all such mutual grievances, injuries and wrongs, *there was no way but only by growing*

into composition and agreement amongst themselves,
by ordaining some kind of government public, and
by yielding themselves subject thereunto; *that unto
whom they granted authority to rule and govern, by
them the peace, tranquillity and happy estate of the
rest might be procured.*" Men always knew that
they might defend themselves and their own commodity against force and injury; and that no man
might in reason determine and assert, partial to
himself, his own right; and, therefore, that "strifes
and troubles would be endless, *except they gave their
common consent all to be ordered by some whom they
should agree upon; without which consent there were
no reason that one man should take upon him to be
lord or judge over another;* because, although there
be according to the opinion of some very great and
judicious men a kind of natural right in the noble,
wise, and virtuous, to govern them which are of
servile disposition; nevertheless for the manifesta-
tion of this their right, and men's more peaceable
contentment on both sides, *the assent of them also
who are to be governed seemeth necessary.*" Hooker
then derives, as did Aristotle, the institution of
kingship from the analogy of fatherhood in private
families. But of kings as the first kind of governors,
he remarks—"not having the natural superiority
of fathers, their power must needs be either usurped,
and then unlawful; or, if lawful, then either granted
or consented unto by them over whom they exercise
the same, or else given extraordinarily from God,

unto whom all the world is subject." That, however, he more than questions the validity of the extraordinary or supernatural derivation of power is indicated by the stringency of the test to which he always subjects it, "by consent of men or *immediate appointment* of God." And in his conclusion the latter alternative seems utterly to vanish: "Howbeit not this [the kingship] the only kind of regiment that hath been received in the world. The inconveniences of one kind have caused sundry other to be devised. So that in a word *all public regiment of what kind soever seemeth evidently to have risen from deliberate advice, consultation and composition between men,* judging it convenient and behoveful; there being no impossibility in nature considered by itself [i. e., before its corruption], but that men might have lived without any public regiment. . . ." [1]

5. Tyranny Indefensible; Aristodemocracy.—"The case of man's nature standing therefore as it doth, some kind of regiment the Law of Nature doth require; yet the kinds thereof being many, Nature tieth not to any one, but leaveth the choice as a thing arbitrary. At first . . . it may be that nothing was further thought upon for the manner of governing, but all permitted unto their wisdom which were to rule, till by experience men found this for all parts very inconvenient. . . . *They saw that to live by one man's will became the cause of all*

[1] Polity, 190-191.

men's misery. This constrained them to come unto
laws, wherein all men might see their duties before-
hand, and know the penalties of transgressing
them.[1] . . . Laws do not only teach what is good,
but they enjoin it, they have in them a certain constraining force. . . . *Most requisite therefore it is
that to devise laws which all men shall be forced to obey
none but wise men be admitted.* Laws are matters of
principal consequence; men of common capacity
and but ordinary judgment are not able (for how
should they?) to discern what things are fittest for
each kind and state of regiment. . . . Even they
which brook it worst that men should tell them of
their duties, when they are told the same by a law,
think very well and reasonably of it. For why?
*They presume that the law doth speak with all indif-
ferency; that the law hath no side-respect to their persons; that the law is as it were an oracle proceeding
from wisdom and understanding.*[2] . . . By the natural law whereunto God hath made all subject,
*the lawful power of making laws to command whole
politic societies of men belongeth so properly unto the
same entire societies, that for any prince or potentate*
of what kind soever upon earth *to exercise the same
of himself*, and not either by express commission
immediately and personally received from God
[Imagine the smile with which Hooker regards that
burden of proof!], *or else by authority derived at the*

[1] Polity, 191–192.
[2] Polity, 193.

*first from their consent upon whose persons they impose
the laws, it is no better than mere tyranny.*" [1]

6. Representative Government.—"Laws they are
not therefore which public approbation hath not
made so. But approbation not only they give who
personally declare their assent by voice, sign, or
act, but also when others do it in their names by
right originally at the least derived from them. *As
in parliaments, councils, and the like assemblies, although we be not personally ourselves present, notwithstanding our assent is by reason of other agents there
in our behalf.* . . . Laws therefore human, of what
kind soever, are available by consent."

As for the filling of offices the following is significant not only as an instance of somewhat amusing
practical wisdom but as indication of the author's
reverence for the principle of degree dependent upon
merit in the administration of a democratic commonwealth: "Where the multitude beareth sway, laws
that shall tend unto preservation of that state must
make common smaller offices to go by lot, for fear
of strife and division likely to arise; by reason that
ordinary qualities sufficing for discharge of such
offices, they could not but by many be desired; . . .
at an uncertain lot none can find themselves grieved,
on whomsoever it lighteth. *Contrariwise the greatest,
whereof but few are capable, to pass by popular election,*
that neither the people may envy such as have those
honors, inasmuch as themselves bestow them, and

[1] Polity, 194.

that the chiefest may be kindled with desire to exercise all parts of rare and beneficial virtue, knowing they shall not lose their labor by growing in fame and estimation amongst the people: *if the helm of government be in the hands of a few of the wealthiest, that then laws providing for continuance thereof must make punishment of contumely and wrong offered unto any of the common sort sharp and grievous.*" [1]

As for monarchies, especially the English monarchy and the power of supreme jurisdiction there, let the reader turn to the eighth book of the Polity— not printed before the author's death in 1600, but undoubtedly known to Sandys and Cranmer, Southampton and his associates—and there he will find, "The axioms of our regal government are these *lex facit regem . . .* and *rex nihil potest nisi quod jure potest.*" The law commands the king.

7. The Right of Revolution.—"Laws therefore human," as Hooker has said above, "of what kind soever, are available by consent." That is to say laws positive, which vary according to external necessity and expediency. Under such positive laws are included all the forms of government, and the forms are therefore alterable according to circumstances. *Laws natural,* on the other hand are "*eternal and immutable. . . .* But men *naturally* have no full and perfect power to command whole politic multitudes of men, therefore utterly without our consent we could in such sort be at no man's com-

[1] Polity, 194–196.

mandment living. And to be commanded we do consent, when that society whereof we are part hath at any time before consented, without revoking the same after by the like universal agreement." [1] . . . And again, "The public power of all societies is above every soul contained in the same societies. And the principal use of that power is to give laws unto all that are under it; *which laws in such case we must obey, unless there be reason showed which may necessarily enforce that the law of Reason or of God doth enjoin the contrary.*" [2] In other words the right to alter the form of government resides in the society which by consent set up the government and publicly approved the laws by which that government should rule.

The rationalistic doctrines of Hooker "were to become soon the most effective weapons in the arsenal of those who were assailing the church and the throne." [3] In them we find not only the germ of Sandys's speeches of 1606 and 1614 in Parliament, of his denunciation of divine right, his insistence upon the elective basis of authoritative power, the consent of the governed, the rational and popular sources of law, its binding force upon king as well as subject, the natural and moral justification of revolution against tyranny; but also the definite

[1] Polity, 194.
[2] Polity, 228.
[3] Wm. A Dunning, Political Theories from Luther to Montesquieu, 210.

principles underlying the charters of steadily increasing liberality achieved by Sandys and his fellow patriots for our forefathers in the American colonies. We have here the formulated concept and sometimes even the verbal basis of the most pregnant utterances of the American Declaration of Independence, and the rationale of certain provisions in the Constitution. Hooker's phrases have lived on to us because of their grave and humble majesty. His argument has lived on to us because in the long struggle for English freedom that began in his day and ended with his disciple, John Locke, in the Revolution of 1688, it was the accepted philosophical justification of the civil rights and liberties, the due process of law, and the prerogative of the Commons, extorted in the thirteenth century by Magna Charta, and reasserted in the fourteenth under Edward III.

The accountability of king to people and their right to withdraw power from a tyrant had indeed, even earlier, been enunciated by Wyclif in the reign of Richard II. The origin of kingly power in the consent of the people had been latent in the fifteenth century De Laudibus Legum of Fortescue. He derived from God "the Law of Nature, to which civil laws are only auxiliary," and for him, the king's power was not absolute, but limited by the law. The Utopia of Sir Thomas More had in 1516 not only "assigned the sovereignty to the people" but had assumed "that society might be conceived in some radically different form." By Bishop Ponet in 1536, though for him as for Aristotle the State is not the outcome of convention but itself a natural and necessary institution, the right of revolution had been asserted—and even that of tyrannicide. By Sir Thomas Smith, in The English Commonwealth of 1583, the omnipotence of Parliament had been laboriously expounded. Meanwhile in Scotland, the national sentiment that the king holds from the people the right to rule and that, if he rules unworthily, the people may depose him, had been expressed by John Major as early as 1521; and more explicitly and vehemently by his pupils, Knox and Buchanan: the former in the outline of his Second Blast, about 1559, and the latter in De Jure Regni, 1579. By Buchanan indeed the fundamental premises of Hooker had been anticipated, for he finds the origin of community in the instinct of nature, and the succeeding origin of the State in "the discords of men, which made it necessary to choose a king." The king's authority, moreover, he derives from the law: the king is not absolute, and if wicked he should be cut off.[1]

But it was by Hooker that the philosophical sequence of the social compact, now abandoned by political thinkers, but in its age and for its purpose most efficient, was first logically developed. Here

---

[1] See Sir Frederick Pollock, History of the Science of Politics, Humboldt Library, No. 42, pp. 22, 26; and G. P. Gooch, The History of English Democratic Ideas in the Seventeenth Century, 32, 34, 42, 47.

first we have the full process of argument: the "state
of nature" in which men are in a "relation of equality," governed by the "law of nature" which is the
law of the "God of nature",—a "law eternal and
immutable" under which men are capable of en-
joying their natural rights of "peace, tranquillity,
and happy estate;" man inwardly averse to the
"sacred laws of his nature," and falling into strife;
the institution of government and of positive law,
with the transition to civil society for the maintenance of these rights.   It is with Hooker that the
original contract between king and people first takes
distinct shape; that the origin of government is in
express terms referred to "deliberate advice, consultation, and composition between men;" its just
powers derived from "common consent all to be
governed by some whom they should agree upon—
without which consent there were no reason that
one man should take upon him to be lord or judge
over another;" its laws positive declared to be of
public approbation and of force with monarch as
well as subject; under such positive laws, "all the
forms of government included, and the forms therefore alterable according to circumstances."   In
Hooker we find the constant implication, if not
enunciation, that in the people is vested this right
of altering the government when the government
"is no better than mere tyranny;" in Hooker, too,
the justification of "other kinds of regiment less
inconvenient than kingship:" of the commonwealth

"where the multitude beareth sway"—of representative government and popular election. And in Hooker we find the insistence upon choice of officials not for birth or station, or by privilege royally bestowed, but for "degree" of merit and peculiar fitness. This is the order of degree consistently emphasized by his contemporary, Shakespeare—the order consistently advocated by Hooker's followers in political philosophy, Harrington, Algernon Sidney, and Locke. It is the aristodemocracy of Washington, Hamilton, and John Adams—"the aristocracy," nobly phrased by Jefferson, "of virtue and talent, which nature has wisely provided for the direction of the interests of society, and scattered with equal hand through all its conditions," an aristocracy deemed essential to a well-ordered republic.[1]

Through the colonial charters achieved by Hooker's parliamentary disciples and Shakespeare's patriot friends of the Virginia Company, through the Petition of Right, through the Convention of January, 1689, with its solemn assertion of the "original contract between king and people," through the succeeding Bill of Rights, and immediately through John Locke's Treatise of Civil Government, Hooker's political conceptions found their way into the mind and speech of James Otis, Franklin, Patrick Henry, Samuel and John Adams, of Jefferson—and so into the Declaration of Independence. I said, immedi-

[1] Jefferson's Writings (Autobiography), I, 36. Ed. 1853.

ately, through John Locke; for his Treatise of 1690 was profoundly and widely studied by the fathers of the American Revolution, and is confessedly a reasoned elaboration of Hooker's ideas of civil polity. The extent of the indebtedness of Locke has been frequently overlooked, and his fundamental doctrine traced to other sources. For instance to Grotius. But Grotius was only seventeen years of age, and had written nothing upon law, when Hooker died. It was no doctrine first formulated at a later date by the Dutch jurist and founder of international law that Locke was espousing when he "declared the law of nature to be a determining body of rules for the conduct of men in their natural condition," or when he maintained that "under this law, of which reason is the interpreter, equality is the fundamental fact in men's relations to one another." Nor was it on a foundation first laid by Grotius that "Locke constructed his doctrine as to the natural rights which belong to every man in the pre-political state." Locke's conception of the state of nature as a pre-political rather than a pre-social condition, a state in which peace and reason and equality prevail, is derived directly from Richard Hooker. In fact Grotius himself was influenced by Hooker. Hooker's conception and exposition of natural law place him in the group of Protestant thinkers who opened the way for Grotius.[1]

[1] Dunning, The Political Philosophy of John Locke, in Pol. Sci. Quart., XX, 230; and his Political Theories from Luther to Montesquieu, 210.

As Hooker thought, so Locke. And the Declaration of Independence echoes the sentiment and phrase of both: "To assume . . . the separate and equal station to which the laws of nature and of nature's God entitle them. . . . We hold these truths to be self evident: that all men are created equal; that they are endowed by their Creator with inalienable rights; that among these are life, liberty, and the pursuit of happiness; that to secure these rights, governments are instituted among men, deriving their just powers from the consent of the governed; that whenever any form of government becomes destructive of these ends it is the right of the people to alter or abolish it. . . . Governments long established should not be changed for light and transient causes. . . . But when a long train of abuses and usurpations, pursuing invariably the same object, evinces a design to reduce them under absolute despotism, it is their right, it is their duty to throw off such government, and to provide new guards for their future security." The cardinal doctrines are in direct descent from Hooker's enunciation of them.

Jefferson was right when he said that "the ball of the Revolution received its first impulse, not from the actors in the event, but from the first colonists." He might well have added: "and from the Jacobean protagonists of colonial rights, their brothers in England; from the word oft reiterated in Parliament by Sandys and Selden and Brooke,

by Phillips, Neville, Sackville, and Digges; from the
motive and deed of Southampton and Cavendish
and the other Patriots of the Virginia Company;
and from their instructor in the principles of equal
opportunity, self-government, justice, and liberty—
the Elizabethan Greatheart of the Anglican Church,
the most judicious political philosopher of the Shakespearian age, the friend of Shakespeare's friends—
Richard Hooker."

CHAPTER VI

SHAKESPEARE'S VIEWS OF THE INDIVIDUAL IN RELA-
TION TO THE STATE

THESE being the political views of the philosopher
who most influenced the founders and the reasserters
of American freedom, what were those of the supreme dramatist of Hooker's day? That Shakespeare
was acquainted with more than one of the so-called
"patriots" of the latter years of Queen Elizabeth,
and friendly with others who joined the survivors
of that Essex uprising and devoted themselves,
under the leadership of Sandys and Southampton,
to measures of constitutional reform during the
reign of King James, we have already seen. We
have seen also that several of these friends and acquaintances of Shakespeare were foremost in the
liberal movement instituted by the Virginia Council
for the government of the young plantation; and
that the poet was not ordinarily informed, but con-
fidentially, of their affairs, and of the disasters and
political difficulties that well nigh wrecked their
purposes. With such knowledge on our part as a
background we may profitably examine the poet's
utterances for some indication of his views concerning political matters, and of the moral and social
principles underlying. Is there in his poems any

such indication? If he took to heart at all the realities of life we should expect to find somewhere in the poems some revelation of his measure of man as a moral and social individual. If "the end" of playing is, indeed, "to hold as 'twere, the mirror up to nature; to show virtue her own feature, scorn her own image, and the very age and body of the time his form and pressure," we should expect to find in Shakespeare's plays something of that contemporary form and pressure; some index of his discrimination between virtue and vice, between the essential and ephemeral in matters moral and social and in the political movements of his period.

"Shakespeare was like putty," says Professor Mackail,[1] quoting from "a forgotten artist of the last century—'Shakespeare was like putty to everybody and everything: the willing slave, pulled out, patted down, squeezed anyhow, clay to every potter. But he knew by the plastic hand what the nature of the moulder was.'" The words rankle; and so too, perhaps, Professor Mackail's approbation of them—"Startling clearness in four words: 'Shakespeare was like putty.'" There are half-truths startling and delusive, and epigrams at once brilliant and opaque. Shakespeare would have smiled. Has not Hamlet forestalled the comparison and its inevitable even if unintended innuendo in his dictum of the end of playing? To show "the very age and body of the time his form and pressure"

[1] Shakespeare after Three Hundred Years, 8, 9.

implies a something more than the passivity of
"clay to every potter." It implies a discrimination
between the sham and the substance, between the
evanescent and the durable, between the mass and
the meaning. It implies more than submission to
every "plastic hand:" it implies discrimination
between botcher and fashioner. It implies more
than a knowledge of "the nature of the moulder:"
it implies an ability "to show" what is moulded.
It implies, above all, the creative power of sublima-
tion: virtue custom-blurred resumes her radiant and
immortal feature; scorn shrivels before the image
of her vice. The difference between putty and
poetry is one of insight, choice, creativity: that is
to say, of truth, worth and beauty. "Shakespeare's
preëminence," as Sir Sidney Lee has said, "resides
in his catholic sensitiveness to external impressions,
and in his power of transmuting them in the crucible
of his mind into something richer and rarer than
they were before." [1] In the transmutation is the
revelation not only of their truth, but of their significance both for Shakespeare and for us. May
we not, without prejudicing the issue by any effort,
here, at tracing the poet's indebtedness to anyone,
aim to discover what Shakespeare regarded as true
and significant concerning the worth of life, especially in the social and political relation of the
individual to the state? The reader who has familiarized himself with the thought of Hooker and

[1] Shakespeare and the Italian Renaissance, 17.

his school may judge whether Shakespeare's way of thinking is of that school if he please.   Whether there is definite resemblance between the poet and the divine we shall consider in the next chapter. The main thing here is to sift out from what is the merely conventional or dramatic utterance of the poet that which is so spontaneous and so variously repeated that it cannot but represent his personal conviction, his heart.

If we had of Shakespeare no residue but his Sonnets, we should know something of his view of life.   If there were no survival but the sixty-sixth of the collection, we should know what values he most highly prized.   For, in that sonnet, neither a mere literary exercise nor an utterance of mechanical adulation, he enumerates the phenomena that he most deplores:

> Tired with all these for restful death I cry,—
> As to behold desert a beggar born,
> And needy nothing trimmed in jollity,
> And purest faith unhappily forsworn,
> And gilded honour shamefully misplaced,
> And maiden virtue rudely strumpeted,
> And right perfection wrongfully disgraced,
> And strength by limping sway disabled,
> And art made tongue-tied by authority,
> And folly, doctor-like, controlling skill,
> And simple truth miscalled simplicity,
> And captive good attending captain ill;—
> Tired with all these, from these I would be gone,
> Save that, to die, I leave my love alone.

With these aspects of contemporary life Shakespeare is tired. From his disapprobation we learn what things make life for him worth living. They are the recognition of merit, irrespective of birth or wealth, merit "trimmed in jollity;" the establishment—in the seats of authority—of honor, right perfection, and the strength that makes for national welfare; freedom of art and speech; the triumph of science over fatuity and pedantry; the conservation of faith and the sacredness of virtue; reverence for truth; goodness controlling evil; and love that, if all the rest were dead, might still make life worth while.

It is, indeed, more than probable that some of Shakespeare's sonnets were exercises of skill, and some, products of conventional adulation. I, for one, hold that all are not to be explained by either premise. With regard to many of them, Wordsworth's judgment cannot be gainsaid; in these "Shakespeare expresses his own feelings in his own person." In others, even though conventional, we find Shakespeare rephrasing positively or negatively one and another of his articles of faith, especially his faith in the worth of spontaneity, of ungilded merit, of truth, of constancy, of virtue,—

> The summer's flower is to the summer sweet,
> Though to itself it only live and die;
> But if that flower with base infection meet,
> The basest weed outbraves his dignity;

his faith in the glory of independence, independence
of popular acclaim or of largess showering from the
stars,—

> Great princes' favourites their fair leaves spread
> But as the marigold at the sun's eye;
> And in themselves their pride lies buried,
> For at a frown they in their glory die.
> The painful warrior famoused for fight,
> After a thousand victories once foil'd,
> Is from the book of honour razed quite
> And all the rest forgot for which he toil'd.

Shall we shrug the shoulder, saying these are but
the commonplaces of a contemporary mode,—these
and the passionate asseverations of the ecstasy,
solace, abiding presence and sufficiency of love, the
tender ideality of self-abnegation in life or death?
Is there no genuineness of personal conviction in
the poet's worship of youth and beauty and of the
truth that is the vital breath of both? and in the
pathos dear to him of their brevity and swift decay?
Is there no poignancy of actual experience in the
recurrent theme of frailty, the insufficiency of the
lust of the flesh, the confession of his own weakness,
and the challenge to his "poor soul?"—

> Poor soul, the centre of my sinful earth . . .
> Buy terms divine in selling hours of dross;
> Within be fed, without be rich no more:
> So shalt thou feed on Death that feeds on men,
> And Death once dead, there's no more dying then.

This unquestioning acceptance of restful Death, Death the gentle, the consoling, the healing, is it in no wise Shakespeare's own acceptance?

Shall we, meticulously sceptical, urge that in all this there is naught but the echo of contemporary fashion, or of the Renaissance Platonism of Italy, or of Ronsard, Jodelle, and Desportes in France? If so, we must also contend that Sir Philip Sidney, who, in his passionate praise of "Stella," lifted many a thought and line from the sonneteers of Italy and France, did not love Stella,—his Penelope Devereux of girlhood, his Lady Rich of married life. But we know that he did love her, and that consumedly. And because Michael Drayton borrowed from the sonnet-sequence of Claude de Pontoux the very name under which he worshipped his "soul-shrined saint," and because he gathered from Ronsard and Desportes flower and fragrance for poetic tribute to her,—the Anne Goodere of his youth, the Lady Rainsford of his after years—shall we say that he did not love her—love her honorably to the day of his death?

The poet-lover may lean upon convention and borrow fantasies from distant sources and sing with ancient echoes. He did in Shakespeare's time. He did in Burns's time. Consciously or not, he sings his love in borrowed strains today. He takes his good where he may find it; the gold is none the less his or hers when laid at the loved one's feet. And so of Shakespeare's attestations of friendship and devotion; so also of his attestations of the essentials of human worth, in personal intercourse or public life. These are Shakespeare, whether they be garbed in appropriated phrase and conventional mode or not. They are Shakespeare if in his sonnets they are his habitual utterance; the more so, if they recur in the fundamental view of life presented by his dramas. Even though expressed in dramatic character, they are Shakespeare when they recur in crises of emotional emergency, and when the conduct of the drama has made clear the universal value to be attached to the emotion. They are Shakespeare if they recur in the prophetic or chorus-like utterance of supernumeraries when the poet does not care to be a dramatist. They are Shakespeare if they recur in soliloquies and asides not vital to the dramatic evolution, or in vital utterances "when the poet forgets to be a dramatist" and, as it were subconsciously, speaks with his own voice. Most unmistakably is that voice Shakespeare's when the creed he utters, or his creatures utter, accords with the temper of the poet as attested by those who knew him,—by Chettle and Weever, Scoloker, Davies of Hereford, Freeman, Heminges and Condell, Ben Jonson, and many another from 1592 to the day of his death and later. To some of those he is the poet of love,—"They burn in love, thy children, Shakespeare het them." To others, he is "friendly Shakespeare," "gentle Shakespeare," "sweet Shakespeare," "so worthy a friend and fellow," "so lovable." "I loved the man," says Jonson, "and do honor his memory (on this side idolatry) as much as any. He was indeed honest and of an open and free nature." To Chettle, "his upright dealing" again, "which argues his honesty," appeals, and also "his civil demeanor;" to Davies of Hereford, his "honesty" again, and his "courage," his generosity "of mind and mood," his "wit," his kingly quality:

> Thou hadst been a companion for a king;
> And been a king among the meaner sort.
> Some others rail; but rail as they think fit,
> Thou hast no railing, but a reigning wit:
> And honesty thou sow'st which they do reap.

For more than one who knew him his estimate of manhood, his appraisal of social honor, of civic duty, and of civil polity, as well as his wisdom and skill, poetry, passion, originality, are manifest in his works,—"Then let thine own works thine own worth upraise." "All that he doth write," cries Leonard Digges, "is pure his own"—

Where Shakespeare lived or spake, Vermin forbear,
Lest with your froth you spot them, come not near . . .
Brief, there is nothing in his wit-fraught Book,
Whose sound we would not hear, on whose worth look
Like old coin'd gold, whose lines in every page
Shall pass true current to succeeding age.

For more than Freeman, Digges, and Ben Jonson, in those works of Shakespeare does Shakespeare's very self appear:

Look how the father's face
Lives in his issue; even so, the race
Of Shakespeare's mind and manners brightly shines
In his well turned and true filed lines:
In each of which he seems to shake a lance,
As brandished at the eyes of Ignorance.

May we not in spite of those who, revolted by the uncritical enthusiasm of the eighteenth century and the idolatry of the early nineteenth, have proceeded to divest the poet of spontaneity, the dramatist of personality, after all recognize a man Shakespeare, a Shakespeare of unborrowed and unassumed thought and passion, and of conviction repeatedly and distinctly uttered? Scepticism is not the only hallmark of scholarship, certainly not of constructive criticism. The philological and historical critics have not been merely destructive: by clearing away the underbrush they have enabled us to see the trees.

II

Shakespeare's ideal of manhood, as prefigured in Sonnet 66, reappears and is reinforced throughout his plays. The personality revealed in the sonnets, and attested by those who spoke with him face to face, illumines in clearer detail and broader sweep the concrete mortals of his mimic world. From the kingdom of vision his creatures step witnessing to his "cloudless, boundless human view." Explicitly or impliedly, not professed but confessed, his human

view is ours to know. It lives in the serious avowal
of the souls that he has created sincere—Hamlets,
Cordelias, Isabellas, Brutuses, Vincentios, Henry
the Fifths; in the jocose or ironical, and therefore
inverted, intimation of the Falstaffs, and the innuendo of jesters, clowns, and fools; in the subacid of
Beatrice and Rosalind; in the perverted and negatively interpretable creed of the Richards, Iagos and
Iachimos; in the throe of action and passion, and in
the cry wrung from the heart of emergency; for
Shakespeare shaped the emergency, thrilled in the
throe, pulsed in the heart of his fashioning.

What, according to Shakespeare's conception, an
Englishman should be (for in spite of clime or time or
garb, all his characters are English at heart) is
somewhat on this wise: in individual and social
relations, first and foremost free and independent,—"every man's soul is his own;" he "bends not
low" nor speaks "in a bondman's key, with bated
breath and whispering humbleness;" he is proud, but
modest withal,—for "whatever praises itself but in
the deed, devours the deed in the praise;" his courage
is fostered by habit, not commandeered by law; he
has the dauntless spirit of resolution; in trial he is as
"one in suffering all, that suffers nothing;" in effort
he has no "traitor doubts" that "make us lose the
good we oft might win by fearing to attempt." His
breastplate is the "heart untainted."

But independence avails him little unless he have
an abiding sense of obligation to the society of which

he forms a part. He is a man of "plain and simple faith," "armed strong in honesty," "precise in promise-keeping," despising deceit—"the seeming truth which cunning times put on to entrap the wisest,"—a man of justice, a man of mercy, a man moving in "the perfect ways of honor," a man who cares not for ceremony, or that scutcheon of honor of which Falstaff talks, that "lives not with the living or the dead." The man after Shakespeare's heart lives as knowing that "no man is the lord of anything till he communicate his parts to others;" that "Nature demands both thanks and use."

But neither independence nor sense of obligation profits unless—and here Shakespeare's humanity becomes humanism—unless one be of well-ordered, well-rounded composition. "Folly and ignorance are the common curse of mankind." But judgment alone, "the pale cast of thought," makes cowards of us; and intellect alone breeds cunning and sophistry to gloze lust and violence with smiles and scripture and artificial tears, to "add colors to the chameleon and set the murderous Machiavel to school." And the man of impulse alone—his "blood will be his direction to his death:" he is but "passion's slave." Shakespeare's man of parts is capable of independence and of service to his fellows, precisely because he is endowed with "large discourse looking before and after" and "God-like reason," and conscience; and because he is blessed with "blood and judgment so well commingled" that he is "not a pipe for Fortune's finger to sound what stop she please."

III

This being somewhat Shakespeare's ideal of manhood in its individual and social relations, what is his thought, implicit or expressed, of the relation of the individual to the state?

Shakespeare was not a prophet, if by prophet we mean one who foresees and foretells the future. If, however, by "prophet" we mean one who interprets aright the conditions of the time, "completely embodying the present in which the future is contained," perceiving in the Ygdrasil of history not merely the branches of good and evil, but the potencies sure to leaf, sure to bud and flower and seed,— if that is what we mean, then Shakespeare was a prophet: a seer, an instinctive sage, an unprofessed political philosopher, of observation, of reflection, of common sense. As in his religious outlook there is— to avail ourselves of Carlyle—"no narrow superstition, harsh asceticism, intolerance, fanatical fierceness, or perversion;" but yet "a Revelation, so far as it goes," of the "thousand-fold hidden beauty and divineness dwelling in all Nature, which let all men worship as they can," so in his outlook upon political life, though he was in "every way an unconscious man, conscious of no heavenly message," there is a revelation of truth which, because visible in his day, is still truth and visible for all days.

He was, as has been frequently said, not in the modern sense democratic. How could he be? Representative government was not yet firmly established: it had not vindicated many of the rights which belonged to it by precedent, still less begun to assert the constitutional authority that it exercises today. And as for pure democracy, or mobocracy, even if one had envisaged for Shakespeare a perfectibility of the Anglo-Saxon race in moral character, in mental sanity, in political wisdom, in unselfish devotion to the common control of common interests, how could he with his sanity, his perception of "the common curse of mankind," have accepted the vision as other than an insubstantial pageant? The populace of his ken was unguided, lacking civil polity and responsibility, unity of national interest, devotion to moral ideas and historical precedent. Though he had faith in, and sympathy with, the sterling virtues of the individual Englishman, his knowledge of English history, as well as his experience of the workings of the contemporary mob, justified a profound distrust of the political functions of any mob—by and for all. Flat democracy, triumphant, directly legislating, unselfishly and consistently, by native impulse and universal ballot—initiative, referendum, and recall— for common as well as individual interests, and honorably administering the affairs of a nation at home and abroad, he would distrust if he were living today. But to representative government, so far as it existed in his day—the government of all, for all, by the best among them, by those who had with distinction studied and achieved the advantage of the state—to such aristocratic republicanism, every line that he has written of king or peer, politician, burgess, or peasant in relation to the state, shows that he yielded his whole-hearted allegiance.

While he repudiates "the many-headed multitude" as politically inconstant, undeliberative, the dupe of the demagogue, he is not unfriendly to the man of low degree as such.

As a playwright he of course adapts himself not only to the immediate intelligence and favor of those for whom he writes but to the changing temper of the day. "In the follies of his mobs, as in the sarcasms of his aristocrats," says Mr. Mackail with an admirable suggestiveness, "he reflects the spirit of his audience whether at Whitehall or at the Bankside. It is only a further exemplification of this that in his later work the tone changes, and he sounds in Lear and elsewhere the note of passionate pity for the poor. That note is his swift response to the ground-swell of the new democracy. The Tudor dynasty had become extinct, and with it the iron Tudor system of repression and reaction had come to an end; the revolutionary movements of the Stuart period were beginning to stir. In these later plays, as in the earlier, Shakespeare is still giving out what he received; he makes vocal, personifies, vitalizes the impressions of his actual environment." True, this, so far as it goes. Shakespeare gives out what he received; but from the impressions that he receives, he selects. Shakespeare personifies and vitalizes; but the vitality that he confers is the vitality of poetry—which is a more philosophical and a higher thing than history, for it tends to express the universal. What spirit of the audience he reflects, he polarizes and purifies. When he responds to the ground-swell of the new democracy, the response is of his heart. When he makes vocal the murmur of the age, the voice is his own. When, in the sonnet which we have quoted, he cries for restful death rather than "behold desert a beggar born" and "gilded honor shamefully misplaced," his heart is speaking. And it is his voice that we hear in the lament of Lucrece,—

> The orphan pines while the oppressor feeds;
> Justice is feasting while the widow weeps.

So, too, in the plays at a later period. When Hamlet soliloquizes:

> For who would bear the whips and scorns of time,
> The oppressor's wrong, the proud man's contumely, . . .
> The insolence of office, and the spurns
> That patient merit of the unworthy takes,
> When he himself might his quietus make,

it is the heart of Shakespeare that responds to the ground-swell, the voice of Shakespeare that expresses "the higher thing than history." When Lear recognizes in the beggars on the country-side brethren of

his misery, the note of passionate pity is no phono-
graphic regurgitation of impressions mechanically
registered:

> Poor naked wretches, wheresoe'er you are,
> That bide the pelting of this pitiless storm,
> How shall your houseless heads and unfed sides,
> Your loop'd and window'd raggedness, defend you
> From seasons such as these? O, I have ta'en
> Too little care of this! Take physic, pomp;
> Expose thyself to feel what wretches feel,
> That thou mayest shake the superflux to them,
> And show the Heavens more just.

Through the lips of the outcast king, Shakespeare's
humanity speaks. It is because the mutable rank-
scented many are to Coriolanus, "You, common cry
of curs," it is because he thinks of them as if he
"were a God to punish, not a man of their infirmity,"
that Coriolanus goes to his fate. While Shakespeare
laughs indeed at the foibles of the crowd, he satirizes
the vanities and the follies of the rich as well and
arraigns the oppressive tyranny and arrogance of a
heartless oligarchy. He is neither communist nor
social democrat, born out of season. Nor is he a
proponent of the aristocratic or monarchic rule that,
deriving from birth or wealth or princes' favor arrays
itself in insolence and ceremony and, seeking its
own end and ease before that of the State manipu-
lates the multitude. For a Brutus of noble though
ill-timed ideals, but of tender heart for the rude and

suffering peasantry, he has naught but pity and admiration.

Shakespeare was not anti-democratic, but like the sanest political thinkers of his day—the Hookers, Sandyses, Seldens, Southamptons, and the colonial builders of Virginia and New Plymouth,—"aristo-democratic." That coinage I should not use had not the adequate "aristocratic" lost in common parlance its wholesome and primal significance, and dwindled to connote a single property of hereditary and titled caste. It has been said that "Shakespeare's whole reading of history is aristocratic." True; but not, as Hazlitt and Whitman conceived, anti-popular and feudal. If we apply the word "aristocratic" to his ideal of government we must invest it with its true intent, of government by the best—that which Plato had in mind when he described the ideal state as one in which wisdom, courage, temperance, and justice obtain and are administered for the happiness of all by guardians selected from all, for their superior fitness, their excellence. Shakespeare was writing his Julius Cæsar at just the time when patriots whom he knew were revolting with Essex against "the iron Tudor system of repression." He was writing his Hamlet, with its dilemma of duty in suspense, the year after Essex had been executed, and while Southampton was in the Tower. He was writing his Lear when Sandys and Southampton were organizing the movement for democracy which stayed not even with

the downfall of the Stuarts. He wrote his Coriolanus
about the time that Sandys, Southampton, and
Brooke were combating both autocratic injustice
and communistic disorder in Virginia, and were
achieving the first free charter for the colony.

Shakespeare is particularly, as Bagehot has told
us, the poet of personal nobility. And nobility to
Shakespeare is "in the last resort a matter of character rather than of descent. He insists, it is true,
upon obedience of word and deed to prescribed authority, and that authority in his world was, as a
matter of fact, vested in kings and princes, but
none the less his root-principle is that of *noblesse
oblige.*" [1] Such nobility the King in All's Well that
Ends Well graciously expounds:

From lowest place when virtuous things proceed,
The place is dignified by the doer's deed:
Where great additions swell's, and virtue none,
It is a dropsied honour. . . . That is honour's scorn,
Which challenges itself as honour's born
And is not like the sire. Honours thrive
When rather from our acts we them derive
Than our foregoers.

With what frequency does the poet indulge in soliloquy (sometimes appropriate to character and
occasion, sometimes not) of unfitness and corruption
in high estate! "For who shall go about," reflects

[1] E. de Sélincourt, English Poets and the National Ideal, 11,
13.

the Prince of Arragon in Portia's casket-room at Belmont,

> Who shall go about
> To cozen fortune and be honourable
> Without the stamp of merit? Let none presume
> To wear an undeservèd dignity.
> O, that estates, degrees, and offices
> Were not derived corruptly, and that clear honour
> Were purchased by the merit of the wearer!
> How many then should cover that stand bare!
> How many be commanded that command!
> How much low peasantry would then be gleaned
> From the true seed of honour! And how much honour
> Picked from the chaff and ruin of the times
> To be new-varnished!

All this from one who has been sneering at "the fool multitude" and is about to be presented with a fool's head because, though deeming wisely of those who should wear dignity, he unwisely deems himself one such. This passage, with its emphasis upon degree and honor "purchased by the merit of the wearer," was written the year, or the year after, Hooker's Ecclesiastical Polity, which makes the same plea, had appeared. And the passage of like spirit in All's Well is of the same period.

As for kings, why spend words to demonstrate what every reader of Shakespeare must see for himself? The poet believes neither in vassalage nor divine right. It is only kings like the ineffectual and histrionic, sentimental and tyrannous Richard II,

who has sucked the life-blood of his realm, that
boast, "Not all the water in the rough rude sea Can
wash the balm off from an anointed king. . . . The
deputy elected by the Lord." Only such, that circle
themselves with glorious angels in God's heavenly
pay; only such, or criminals who, like Claudius,
have won a throne by murder and would by murder
hold it, that hedge themselves with divinity. Solely
to buttress a ruined cause—foreseeing the civil disasters that follow dethronement without due trial
by one's peers—do prelates, like King Richard's
Bishop of Carlisle, put forward the current hy-
pothesis of the divine right of kings. Quite other,
the wisdom of John of Gaunt: "God's substitute.
His deputy anointed in his sight" becomes, by crime,
God's quarry; when the monarch commits his
anointed body to the cure of flatterers, and leases
out his England "like to a tenement or pelting
farm," and makes the state of law a "bondslave to
the law," he deposes himself. The tragedy of so-
called divine right pervades Shakespeare's historical plays,—the tragedy of mortal pretension
vain in itself, destructive and pitiable when coupled
with self-devotion, incompetence, unfaithfulness,
unscrupulousness, disloyalty to the realm, to the
people. For ruler and ruled are one people. The
people, though yet unconscious of it, are sovereign
and in them resides whatever divine right there be.
Hooker and the leaders of the nascent liberal movement in England were not unconscious of that. Nor

was Shakespeare: his historical plays are a body-blow to the theory of the divine right of kings.

Something of the characteristics a king should not have, of the graces he should, we read in the colloquy between Macduff and the prince whom he summons to the realm as its rightful savior from oppression—truest issue of the throne. To Malcolm professing vices that he has not, lust and stanchless avarice, Macduff replies,—

> Boundless intemperance
> In nature is a tyranny: it has been
> The untimely emptying of the happy throne,
> And fall of many kings;

and then, "This avarice . . . hath been the sword of our slain kings." What "the king-becoming graces" are, the prince, disclaiming them with politic pretence, recites:

> Justice, verity, temperance, stableness,
> Bounty, perseverance, mercy, lowliness,
> Devotion, patience, courage, fortitude.

The play celebrates the coming to England of the Malcolm's royal line, the fancied hope of Southampton and other of Shakespeare's friends. But with what unconscious prophetic irony is the play invested! The vices professed may not have been those of all four Stuart pretenders to divine right. But neither were the virtues; and twice in the Stuart career was England to witness "the untimely emptying of the happy throne."

The reciprocal responsibility of prince and subject in allegiance to the commonwealth is a prime lesson of The Life of Henry V. With all his faults of historical verisimilitude and Shakespearian limitation, Shakespeare's favorite prince is ruler and servant both. He is the soul of a unified people—"such a plain king that thou wouldst think I had sold my farm to buy my crown." He is the representative and instrument of the national consciousness and will. He advances no proprietary claim to God. He is according to his lights (and Shakespeare's) a democratic king:—"For though I speak it to you," says he, masquerading as a private, to privates Bates, Court, and Williams: "though I speak it to you, I think the king is but a man, as I am; the violet smells to him as it doth to me; all his senses have but human conditions; his ceremonies laid by, in his nakedness he appears but a man." Then he continues, "Every subject's duty is the king's; but every subject's soul is his own." Every subject's duty is the king's, for, but for ceremony, the peasant "had the forehand and the vantage of a king."—

> The slave, a member of the country's peace,
> Enjoys it, but in gross brain little wots
> What watch the king keeps to maintain the peace,
> Whose hours the peasant best advantages.

"Every subject's duty is the king's." Whether in the words of Henry V or the loyal Fauconbridge

or Gaunt or the gardener at Langley, every subject—
from peasant to peer all "dear friends" of king and
country—is under obligation to the state.

From those "whose limbs were made in England,"
whose lives of peace have been passed in "modest
stillness and humility," naught else can be expected
when the blast of war blows than that they "stiffen
the sinews, summon up the blood," prove their love
of country, even to the death: they "can not die
anywhere so contented as in the king's company,
his cause being just and his quarrel honorable."
Nay, more, implies our patriot-poet, unflinching:
if none but the patriot-king and his council know
the cause to be spotless, still with them marches the
obligation of the subject. "Every man's soul is
his own:" but with individual freedom and responsibility there goes, hand in hand, political duty—
the patriotism of national faith, unity, devotion.
Such patriotism is the premise of Fauconbridge's
assurance:

> Come the three corners of the world in arms,
> And we shall shock them. Nought shall make us rue,
> If England to itself do rest but true.

This obligation of reciprocal responsibility is not,
however, an argued patriotism with Shakespeare;
it is the instinctive patriotism of national pride,
gratitude, and love. Gaunt's apostrophe is not of
the head but the heart:

This royal throne of kings, this sceptred isle,
This earth of majesty, this seat of Mars,
This other Eden, demi-paradise,
This fortress built by Nature for herself
Against infection and the hand of war,
This happy breed of men, this little world,
This precious stone set in the silver sea,
Which serves it in the office of a wall
Or as a moat defensive to a house
Against the envy of less happier lands,
This blessed plot, this earth, this realm, this England, . . .
This land of such dear souls, this dear, dear land,
Dear for her reputation through the world.

Lyrical outbursts of this kind may sound insular;
but to infer that Shakespeare's patriotism was
merely insular is to ignore his absorption of much
that was best in the literature and spirit of the Renaissance, and his sympathy with it. Timely elaboration of the thought is afforded by Sir Sidney Lee.[1]
"Through Shakespeare's lifetime," says he, "Englishmen explored Italy in numbers which increased
year by year. . . . They were impressed not
merely by the country's intellectual and artistic
triumphs, but by the refined amenities of her social
life. . . . 'Homekeeping youth have ever homely
wits.' wrote Shakespeare. A perfect man, he added,
was one who was tried and tutored outside his native
country. The dramatist laughingly detected in
the travelled Englishman no worse failing than a

[1] Shakespeare and the Italian Renaissance, 11–18.

predilection for outlandish manners and dress which offended insular taste. . . . A large part of Italian poetry and prose of the Renaissance was accessible to him in English translation. . . . I claim Shakespeare as the greatest of humanists in the broad sense which the term justly bears in the history of the Italian Renaissance." . . . But, continues Sir Sidney, "he cannot be suspected of cosmopolitanism in its undesirable significance. The bracing air of toleration fed his spirit; but that virtuous sustenance never impaired his love of his own country or his confident faith in her destiny. It was he who apostrophized his country and countrymen in his own magnificent diction as 'This happy breed of men, this little world . . . This blessed plot, this earth, this realm, this England.' At the same time Shakespeare, with almost equal fervor, deprecates the shortness of vision which ignores the patriotism of other countries, and refuses all fellow-feeling with them:

> Hath Britain all the sun that shines? Day, night,
> Are they not but in Britain? . . . Prithee, think
> There's livers out of Britain.

Shakespeare is at once the noblest expositor of patriotism, and the most resolute contemner of insularity."

IV

Our poet's political philosophy, if such we may term his imaginative interpretation of history and of legal and political theory, is based, like that of the greatest philosopher of all time, upon justice, fraternity of effort, allegiance.

His justice is not of legal quibble. Though Chief Justice Campbell expressed his astonishment at the poet's acquaintance with legal technicalities, Shakespeare's knowledge of the law was "neither profound nor accurate," nor was it more in evidence than that of many contemporary sonnetteers and dramatists. However acquired—by contact with its procedure in his own lawsuits and in those of his family and neighbors, or by intercourse with the members of his social circle in the Inns of Court, or by absorption of the litigious atmosphere of his day,—his respect for the dignity of law is, with a few exceptions, not discoverable in his portrayal of trial scenes, or in his employment of legal dialectic and phraseology, or in the frequent metaphor and color of the law. "Its solemn absurdities, its quibbling prevarications, its formal futilities tickled Shakespeare's sense of humor." [1] His respect for law is displayed in the treatment of its nobler aspects, moral, positive, divine.

[1] Arthur Underhill in Shakespeare's England, I, 381 *et seq.*, and Review in The Times, Literary Supplement, July 21, 1916.

His justice is of the moral law, the same for dynasty and for nation as for individual. It is of cumulative fate or fortune, *Moira*, "visiting the sins of
the fathers upon the children unto the third and
fourth generation of those that hate God, and showing mercy unto thousands of them that love him
and keep his commandments." This is the moral
teaching of his Histories, when regarded in their
chronological sequence from the origins of family
strife in Richard II to the reconciliation of the war-
ring factions at the end of Richard III. The Histories afford not only the spectacle of innocent
suffering and of just retribution in careers proceeding to catastrophes fraught with both pity and
fear, but also the spectacle of inherited tendencies
descending the generations with boon as well as
retributive bane. The sequence thus mitigates the
aspect of inexplicable catastrophe, essential to the
highest kind of tragedy: it reasserts justice as mercy
in the careers of many whose characteristics, inherited
or acquired, are in conformity with the welfare of the
corporate movement. Likewise, in serious application to the individual irrespective of heredity, his
law is that of "poetical justice unknown" as Professor Mackail has said "to any court or code."
Shakespeare's justice is also of law positive in its
nobler function,—"all-binding, keeping form and
due proportion," even-handed in execution. "Go,
bind thou up yon dangling apricocks"—says the
gardener of Langley in that immortal idyllic inter-

scene of Richard II where Shakespeare's sheer
imagination plays:

> Go, bind thou up yon dangling apricocks,
> Which, like unruly children, make their sire
> Stoop with oppression of their prodigal weight;
> Give some supportance to the bending twigs.
> Go thou, and like an executioner,
> Cut off the heads of too fast growing sprays,
> That look too lofty in our commonwealth;
> All must be even in our government.
> You thus employed, I will go root away
> The noisome weeds, which without profit suck
> The soil's fertility from wholesome flowers.

The poet's justice is also of law divine. God is
"the top of judgment," and of mercy, too: "It is
an attribute to God himself; And earthly power
doth then show likest God's, When mercy seasons
justice." A justice this, of moral authority higher
than the will of earthly judge or monarch or of the
state; a justice of which some glimpse is vouch-
safed to mortals through that "discourse of reason"
with which the Maker has endowed them.

That Shakespeare's philosophy of the state assumes fraternity of effort has appeared from the
foregoing. "We few," says Henry V on the memorable day of Agincourt,"shall be remembered"—

> We few, we happy few, we band of brothers,
> For he to-day that sheds his blood with me
> Shall be my brother.

The state demands not only the devotion of the individual, but the coöperation of·all for common order and .common control. Shakespeare looked back to an England divided against itself and devastated by the Wars of the Roses during an agony of which the cessation was no farther removed from his day or consciousness than are the French Revolution and the Napoleonic wars from ours. Those English civil wars still appealed vividly "to the popular imagination; and the force of tradition was then far more potent than it can ever be in an age of primers." [1] Is it strange that the political moral of his "histories" from the reign of John to that of Richard III, and sometimes of plays remote from England, but dealing with history, is the supreme importance of national concord in affliction as in prosperity? But this national concord is not of flat democracy likely to degenerate into anarchy and then tyranny, but of free coöperation of distinct classes, according to their several degrees of merit and fitness, for the good of the community. It is the polity of a commonwealth or *res publica* advocated by many of Shakespeare's contemporaries and predecessors—the commonwealth that Sir Thomas Smith as early as 1583, or Richard Hooker in 1594, had described as the best kind of democracy. The theory derives directly from consideration of English history but ultimately from the teachings of Plato. In the Republic, says Socrates, "temperance re-

[1] Sir Walter Raleigh, Shakespeare, 40–41.

sembles a concord of harmony . . . producing a
unison between the weakest and the strongest and
the middle." From Plato's Republic Cicero borrowed the analogy; and from Cicero's Republic, of
which we have only fragments, the passage came
to the Elizabethans through St. Augustine's City
of God.[1] "For government," says Shakespeare's
Exeter in Henry V (1599), using almost the words of
St. Augustine's Latin,

> For government, though high and low and lower,
> Put into parts, doth keep in one consent,
> Congreeing in a full and natural close,
> Like music.

And the Archbishop standing by, continues the
thought:

> Therefore doth heaven divide
> The state of man in divers functions,
> Setting endeavour in continual motion,
> To which is fixed as an aim or butt,
> Obedience: for so work the honey-bees,
> Creatures that by a rule in nature teach,
> The act of order to a peopled kingdom.

Then follows that description of the hive—none
the less indicative of Shakespeare's view because perhaps elaborated from Lyly's Euphues,—which with
wondrous wisdom develops the aristodemocratic
ideal of a realm in which all functions and degrees,
the 'emperor" with the rest, play for the common

[1] See H. R. D. Anders, Shakespeare's Books, 278.

service their willing parts. Still more definitely emphasizing the democratic quality of the ruler, the figure recurs in All's Well that Ends Well of 1595–1602, where the king, sickening to death, wishes

> Since I nor wax nor honey can bring home,
> I quickly were dissolved from my hive,
> To give some labourers room.

To this figure of the well-ordered government, with its observance of degrees in duly proportioned subordination of all to the common weal, Shakespeare returns a few years later in his Troilus and Cressida, reinforcing it this time with what looks like an adaptation from Hooker's Ecclesiastical Polity. Here his mouthpiece is Ulysses—

When that the general is not like the hive
To whom the foragers shall all repair,
What honey is expected? Degree being vizarded,
The unworthiest shows as fairly in the mask.
The heavens themselves, the planets, and this centre
Observe degree, priority and place. . . .
Take but degree away, untune that string,
And, hark, what discord follows! Each thing meets
In mere oppugnancy.—

A thought again and again emphasized in the political writings of the Renaissance; a thought so recurrent in divers Shakespearian plays, and so admirably extended beyond the dramatic need, that it impresses us as indubitably the poet's conviction concerning the *sine qua non* of political potency and peace. That the poet does not, however, by the insistence of his Ulysses upon degree, endorse the extreme aristocratic interpretation of degree as bound up with "primogenitive and due of birth," appears from the fact that in the same sequence he includes degrees and laurels compassed not by birth but worth. The political philosophy of England under the Tudors recognized, indeed, the kingly office "as the source from which the various titles of honor and grades in the higher ranks of society spring;" but Shakespeare was not alone in recognizing also a more democratic ideal—in calling for the recognition of merit irrespective of birth, in deploring "right perfection wrongfully disgraced," in calling for government by fraternity of effort. The thought was that of Hooker and Fulke Greville and of the active leaders of the liberal movement from 1594 down.

From disregard of the principles of which we have spoken factions arise: allegiance is vitiated, and the national existence imperilled. In Measure for Measure, of about the same date as the Troilus, the greatest peril to the state proceeds, according to the good but indulgent Duke, from laws "let sleep," from false report and backwounding calumny of those in constituted authority: then "liberty plucks justice by the nose." In 2 Henry VI, compiled earlier, "the commons, like an angry hive of bees That want their leader, scatter up and down

And care not who they sting in his revenge." In
King John, also written earlier, it is because discontented visionaries have been suborned by ˙foreign
cajolery to quarrel with obedience,

> Swearing allegiance and the love of soul
> To stranger blood, to foreign royalty,

that the "inundation of mistempered humor" has
overspread the realm. And it is only when such
"destruction and perpetual shame" have been
pushed "out of the weak door of our fainting land"
that the ever-loyal Fauconbridge, Shakespeare's
patriot of the play, utters his prophetic and not
altogether boastful assurance—

> This England never did, nor never shall,
> Lie at the proud foot of a conqueror,
> But when it first did help to wound itself.

The whole course of our poet's political drama makes
for the development of a national consciousness by
directing the freedom of the individual toward the
service of the common weal and ideal—in coöperation, aristodemocratic according to just degrees of
function and desert, under the moral leadership not
of an autocrat nor an oligarchy but of the best. As
in Richard II and Henry V, so supremely in King
John—plays befitting the critical period in national
affairs, 1594–1599—is the lesson of national unity
Shakespeare's dominant motive. Though even the

lines last quoted are based upon those of an earlier
Fauconbridge in an anonymous play, the poetic
fervor and patriotism in the Life and Death of
King John are Shakespeare's own. To a degree not
paralleled by any contemporary dramatist, and with
an impressiveness one may call unique, King John
is also a lesson in national sovereignty. "Shakespeare is determined to write a drama of which the
hero shall be not a king, but the nation itself; the
genius of a people, as apart from the caprice or the
villainy of its rulers. The people of England, as
impersonated in Fauconbridge are the character
and the theme of King John." [1]

V

Though Shakespeare depicts war as "the son of
Hell;" though, when the wars of the Roses are ended,
Richmond's prayer for "smooth-faced Peace With
smiling Plenty and fair prosperous days" is also
Shakespeare's; though the poet greets the accession
of James I with "Peace proclaims olives of endless
age,"—his is not the peace described by one of his
clowns, "a very apoplexy, lethargy, mull'd, deaf,
sleepy, insensible." "Plenty and peace breeds
cowards," says Imogen. Though Shakespeare has
no sympathy for him who wantonly "comes to open
The purple testament of bleeding war," especially
of civil war, the state as Shakespeare conceived it

[1] Morton Luce, Handbook of Shakespeare's Works, 400–401.

is martially organized to maintain the rights of
peace. He tells us again and again that "the wound
of peace is surety, surety secure." It is not sufficient
that his England, crowning her brows with fillets
of prosperity and indolence, pour mingled wine to
Destiny. She shall be not empty of defense but
provident as of war in expectation and, with the
unquestioning coöperation of her subjects, impreg-
nable, "still secure And confident from foreign purposes." In times of peace such as our modern world
recently enjoyed while international sanctions obtained or seemed to obtain, Shakespeare's contempt
of "less happier lands" and suspicion of their "envy"
might savor of chauvinism. But in his day the
confidence even of statesmen in international pro-
fessions of amity was not ordinarily deeper than that
of his Henry V or his Fauconbridge. If he had
heard as much of international promises as we have,
and could judge of their worth in certain mouths
now, his patriotism, even his chauvinism would, I
venture to say, be precisely what they were. In
his comparatively unenlightened condition he undoubtedly held, with his own Lymoges, "The peace
of heaven is theirs that lift their swords In . . .
just and charitable war." As for checks and disasters, when his Agamemnon reminds the allied
princes, abashed because "after seven years' siege
yet Troy walls stand," that deterrents are not shame,
it is Shakespeare who holds that they "are indeed
nought else"

But the protractive trials of great Jove
To find persistive constancy in men;
The fineness of which metal is not found
In fortune's love; for then the bold and coward,
The wise and fool, the artist and unread,
The hard and soft, seem all affin'd and kin.
But, in the wind and tempest of her frown,
Distinction with a loud and powerful fan,
Puffing at all, winnows the light away;
And what hath mass and matter by itself
Lies rich in virtue and unmingled.

When his Fauconbridge, the sword of the nation once unsheathed, rails on "Commodity" that would draw the realm "From a resolved and honorable war To a most base and vile-concluded peace," it is Shakespeare that rails. We may be sure that, if he were living now, he would be repeating with unction the words of his wag in Measure for Measure, "Heaven grant us its peace, but not the King of Hungary's!"

In his political instincts Shakespeare was, according to his circumstance and insight, a meliorist,—not a theorist, sentimentalist, doctrinaire, political or journalistic ostrich, or gelatinous optimist. He was historically and morally discipled: not a blasphemer of God as pietistic protagonist of selfishness and lethargy. He was not provincially blinded to national honor and obligation. He was not a pacifist at any price. To Shakespeare the imperfectibility of human nature, even with its god-like apprehen-

sion, is self-evident. He looked for amelioration,—
but not through national oblivion of dignity and
right, or international council of angelic hierarchies.
A millennium before the kingdom of God is fulfilled
in every carnal heart, he could no more visualize than
does any sane American today.

When, in writing the speech of Ulysses, quoted
in part above, Shakespeare departs from the Platonic tradition and, adapting Chaucer or Rabelais
or Hooker, or any one of the numerous sources at
his command, portrays the destruction of the heavens
and the earth upon the neglect of law and degree, he
strays at times from the human analogy of the turmoil within the state to that of turmoil between
state and state, nay, even, to that of universal
war:

> But when the planets
> In evil mixture to disorder wander,
> What plagues and what portents! What mutiny!
> What raging of the sea! shaking of earth!
> Commotion in the winds! Frights, changes, horrors,
> Divert and crack, rend and deracinate
> The unity and married calm of states
> Quite from their fixure!

May no lesson for a world of nations be derived from
the poetic vision of what results when, with disregard of justice and due proportion, a planetary
power thus plunges into strife and rends "the married
calm of states?" "Enterprise is sick." "Peaceful

commerce from dividable shores" loses its "authentic place:"

> The bounded waters,
> Should lift their bosoms higher than the shores
> And make   sop of all this solid globe.
> Strength should be lord of imbecility,
> And the rude son should strike his father dead.
> Force should be right; or rather, right and wrong,
> Between whose endless jar justice resides,
> Should lose their names, and so should justice too.
> Then everything includes itself in power,
> Power into will, will into appetite;
> And appetite, an universal wolf,
> So doubly seconded with will and power,
> Must make perforce an universal prey,
> And last eat up himself.

In the last ten lines the poet has returned to the Platonic tradition; but he has transformed the "wolf" of Plato's republic into a Wolf of the World.

Though in Shakespeare's day international law was but in its infancy, for Shakespeare law and humanity rule between states, and over states the justice of God. Henry V, questioning whether with right and conscience he may make a claim on France that if denied shall entail war, conjures his archbishop to unfold justly whether there is a right in law to bar him from the claim: "And God forbid . . . that you should fashion, wrest or bow your reading" with aught "whose right"

Suits not in native colours with the truth;
For God doth know how many now in health
Shall drop their blood in approbation
Of what your reverence shall incite us to.
Therefore take heed how you impawn our person,
How you awake our sleeping sword of war.
We charge you, in the name of God, take heed;
For never two such kingdoms did contend
Without much fall of blood, whose guiltless drops
Are every one a woe, a sore complaint
'Gainst him whose wrong gives edge unto the swords
That make such waste in brief mortality.

Whether the historical Henry was of so nice conscience and humanized ideal, such responsibility for
guiltless bloodshed, matters little. There is nothing
in the sources to show that he was. This humanity
whose guardian and recording angel is Law, is of
the poetic heart and vision of Shakespeare, as is all
that I have quoted in the preceding sections.

VI

Writing of the Age of Elizabeth, Professor Raleigh [1]
has recently said that "the political beliefs and
habits of thought which seem to express themselves
in Shakespeare's plays were the average beliefs of
the time. . . . The English historical plays treat
the clash of personalities, and exhibit human character tested by great events, but hardly touch on
political theory. There is nothing to wonder at in

[1] Sir Walter Raleigh, in Shakespeare's England, I, 7-11.

this; authors and craftsmen who have taken human nature for their province commonly stand aloof from the politics of their age. But the fact is that the political issues which exercised the imagination of the ordinary intelligent man in Shakespeare's day were few and simple. Indeed it might truly be said that there was only one live question, or at least there was only one question so real and insistent and practical that it overshadowed all the rest. That question was how political unity and power might be achieved and consolidated against the forces of anarchy, against domestic treason and foreign aggression. It is the question treated by Machiavel in the wonderful little book which dominated all the political thought of the sixteenth century. But even if the problem of the Prince had never been mooted in literature, it would have been brought home to the minds of men by experience. . . . Under Elizabeth the nation longed for security and peace; the maintenance and security of the powers of government was what concerned the people; and it was not till a later time that the question of the balance and subdivision of political power became the chief problem for thinkers. . . . That the sovereign powers of the State might be exercised by a corporation or council was a possibility which had to be considered by Machiavel, but it was too remote from English thought and habit to claim attention in England. . . . In this matter Shakespeare is simply a man of his time.

He believed in rank and order and subordination. His speeches in favor of these things have nothing ironical about them, and are never answered by equally good speeches on the other side. Indeed they may all be paralleled from the works of his contemporaries." Of "the greatest of Shakespeare's dramatic speeches on politics," that of Ulysses recommending order and subordination, Sir Walter remarks, "Popular orators, from Antony to Jack Cade, who pander to the restless desires of the mob, get from the dramatist no such measure of sympathy as went to the making of this speech. Shakespeare, it is sometimes said, never takes a side. It is true that for the most part he takes his stand with average humanity, and is hardly ever eccentric. But he had a meaning, even while drama was his trade; in this matter of politics he was on the side of the government, and of all but a very few who were proud to call themselves the subjects of the Queen."

With all that is said here concerning Shakespeare's belief in the political unity and power of the state, in rank and order and subordination, I am of course in accord; and I grant that his utterances in this respect may be paralleled from the works of his contemporaries, at least his non-dramatic contemporaries. But I question whether he was, as a subject, always "on the side of the government," especially when the Queen sent Essex to the scaffold and Southampton to the Tower, and when the "Patriots" were remonstrating against the auto-

cratic methods and favoritism of James in 1614.
And I am sure that not all the political beliefs and
habits of thought of Shakespeare were "the average
beliefs of the time." His judgments concerning
autocracy, concerning political unity and the sovereignty of the people, concerning the recognition
of merit in government, the rights of the individual,
the consciousness of justice and not of might in the
administration of foreign as well as domestic relations,
are differentiated from, and are above, "the average
beliefs of the time." They are the judgments of the
wisest and most conscientiously patriotic of his
contemporaries. Especially is this the case in his
treatment of the "problem of the Prince." How
far in this respect Shakespeare's view is lifted above
"the average belief of the time," even in England, is
luminously expressed by a writer on the national
ideal in English poetry. "There can be little doubt,"
says Professor de Sélincourt,[1] "that when Shakespeare drew the portrait" of the ideal ruler in Henry
V "his eye was firmly fixed in reprobation upon
another ideal current at his time, which, though
generally but loosely denounced by his contemporaries, was exercising an indubitable influence upon
statesmen and politicians. That policy was Machiavellianism. Machiavelli's Prince had been the text-
book of Thomas Cromwell, the powerful adviser
of Henry VIII; its precepts were in a measure followed by both Cecil and Leicester; much of its

[1] English Poets and the National Ideal, pp. 30-33.

teaching was advocated later by Lord Bacon.[1]
Shakespeare's delineation of Henry V becomes more
significant when we turn to the pages of Machiavelli and see the political and national teaching to
which Henry is, as it were, the counterblast. The
prime object with which Machiavelli wrote was to
effect the unification of Italy. Hence his idea of
the state is confined to its military and political
aspects; he ignores culture, private comfort and
advantage, and all religious considerations. . . .
He maintained certain propositions, which exercised a fascination over his Elizabethan readers
even while they execrated their author, and particularly over those who were themselves empire-
builders. The first of these is the doctrine that the
end justifies the means; the second that Christianity
does not encourage that idea of worldly glory which
is essential to the welfare, nay, the existence of a
state, whilst Paganism upholds worldly glory as
admirable. . . ." According to Machiavelli the
prince "must not be guided in his actions by the
ordinary moral code. He must love his country
more than the safety of his soul. He must
be careless of the individual and consider only
the glory of the community. Consequently we
find him telling us with care and exactitude, when
the prince should break his word, when he should
betray his servant, when he should throw over an

[1] Who, as I have pointed out in Appendix D, cut his coat to
suit the cloth.

ally he is pledged to support, and so on; and particular emphasis is laid upon the use of fraud to achieve his ends, for 'it behoves the ruler to be a fox as well as a lion.' All this sounds horrible enough in cold blood, but no student of history could affirm that Machiavelli was introducing new ideas into statecraft. He was merely reducing to a science, and setting the seal of political philosophy upon methods which have always played a large part in the policy of kings and governments. Machiavelli was the Treitschke and Bernhardi of the Renaissance. The novelty consisted in the codification, as it were, and the justification of acts which, though often practised, had been regarded hitherto as morally indefensible. It was a clear statement of the superiority of the expedient over the right, a definite and cynical denial that the same laws of morality applied to the state and to the individual, an assertion of the principle that 'necessity knows no law.' Shakespeare's answer to this view of politics is found in all his delineations of political and national life. . . . Shakespeare was no professional political philosopher, he was a practical dramatist and a poet, whose first interest and study was human life and individual human character. But like all Elizabethans he was a patriot who loved to ponder over his nation's history, and this was his reading of history." That his reading of history was by no means that of the average man but that of the ripest thinkers and patriots of his day, has, I trust, already been shown.

They were the men who, fortifying the ramparts of liberty in England, laid also the foundations of liberty in America. The most eminent and immediate of their masters in political philosophy was Richard Hooker.

Like Hooker and his disciple Sandys, like Sandys and Southampton and their associates in the Virginia Council and in parliament, Shakespeare repudiates autocracy whether by divine right or force. Like them he repudiates also mob-rule, communism, and flat democracy. Hooker justifies other kinds of regiment than monarchy; Sandys goes further, and is at heart opposed to government by monarchy: Shakespeare accepts monarchy as the established form of rule in England, but he believes in its constitutional limitation. Hooker and Sandys justify the deposition of the unjust king; so does Shakespeare. Hooker and his disciple Sandys, and Sandys's associates in the Virginia Council and in Parliament, insist upon government by consent of the governed. Shakespeare has no faith in the fitness of all the governed to govern themselves; but he joins hands with Hooker and the patriots of the council and of Parliament in the ideal of a government administered for the people by their fittest— not by an aristocracy of birth or wealth but of merit, an aristodemocracy of *noblesse oblige*. In government thus representative, struggling in his day toward realization, Shakespeare is undoubtedly a believer. Like the thinkers—Hooker and Greville—

like Sandys, Southampton, Pembroke, Neville, Gates, De la Warr, Sackville, Brooke, Cavendish, Selden, Digges, Martin, Hoskyns, the Ferrars, and many other patriots in the Council of the Virginia Company, in Parliament, or in the colony, friends of Shakespeare or friends of his friends, the poet believed in the right of the individual to liberty, property and the pursuit of happiness; in equality before the law; and in law "all-binding, keeping form and due proportion;" in even-handed justice; in duty to the common order in society and state; in fraternity of effort and patriotic allegiance. Like the best of them he affirmed right conscience as arbiter of internal issues; and he believed in a God overruling with justice the affairs of all nations.

Let us now consider more in detail the points of contact between Shakespeare's utterance and that of the philosopher of the liberal movement.

CHAPTER VII

SHAKESPEARE AND HOOKER

SHAKESPEARE's utterances of social and political creed, as quoted in the preceding chapter and as there summed up, are with but few exceptions anticipated by Hooker in his publication of 1594. If the similarity between the twain were merely of thought, and but once or twice apparent in their works, it might be matter of coincidence, explicable by the commonplace of tradition and of literary and conversational currency: Hooker was preaching at the Temple from 1585 to 1591; Shakespeare was in London from 1587 on. But not only is the consentaneity recurrent and, so far as Shakespeare is concerned, widely distributed through his poetic output, the similarity is of figure and language as well; and sometimes it is in marked degree arresting. Hooker's book was deeply studied and profoundly admired by Londoners of political tendency long after his death in 1600. Shakespeare was actively occupied in London for some ten years later than that.

Of the parallelism between these two writers let us take the most extended and diversified example. It is that which I have already in part quoted as illustrating Shakespeare's insistence upon the doctrine of "degree." Says Ulysses, accounting for the Grecian reverses before Troy (Troilus and Cressida, I, iii, 78–137),

> The speciality of rule hath been neglected;
> And, look, how many Grecian tents do stand
> 80 Hollow upon this plain, so many hollow factions.
> When that the general is not like the hive
> To whom the foragers shall all repair,
> What honey is expected? Degree being vizarded,
> The unworthiest shows as fairly in the mask.
> 85 The *heavens themselves, the planets, and this centre*
> *Observe* degree, priority and place,
> *Insisture, course,* proportion, *season,* form,
> Office and custom, in all line of *order;*
> And therefore is the *glorious planet Sol*
> 90 In noble eminence enthroned and *spher'd*
> Amidst the other; whose medicinable eye
> Corrects the ill aspects of planets evil,
> And posts, like the *commandment of a king,*
> Sans check to good and bad. *But when the planets*
> 95 *In evil mixture to disorder wander,*
> *What plagues and what portents!* what mutiny!
> What raging of the sea! *shaking of earth!*
> *Commotion in the winds!* Frights, changes, horrors,
> Divert and crack, rend and deracinate
> 100 The unity and married calm of states
> Quite from their fixure! O, when degree is shak'd,
> Which is the ladder to all high designs,
> Then enterprise is sick! How could communities,
> Degrees in schools, and brotherhoods in cities,

105 Peaceful commerce from dividable shores,
The primogenitive and due of birth,
Prerogative of age, crowns, sceptres, laurels,
But by degree, stand in authentic place?
Take but degree away, untune that string,
110 And, hark, what discord follows! Each thing meets
In mere oppugnancy. The bounded waters
Should lift their bosoms higher than the shores
And make a sop of all this solid globe.
Strength should be lord of imbecility,
115 And the rude son should strike his father dead.
Force should be right; or rather, right and wrong,
Between whose endless jars justice resides,
Should lose their names, and so should justice too.
Then everything includes itself in power,
120 Power into will, will into appetite;
And appetite, an universal wolf,
So doubly seconded with will and power,
Must make perforce an universal prey,
And last eat up itself. Great Agamemnon,
125 This chaos, when degree is suffocate,
Follows the choking.
And this neglection of degree is it
That by a pace goes backward, in a purpose
It hath to climb. The general's disdain'd
130 By him one step below, he by the next,
That next by him beneath; so every step,
Exampled by the first pace that is sick
Of this superior, grows to an envious fever
Of pale and bloodless emulation;
135 And 'tis this fever that keeps Troy on foot,
Not her own sinews. To end a tale of length,
Troy in our weakness stands, not in her strength.

This speech was written at the earliest in 1602, and not later than 1609. The likeness between Shakespeare's thought and expression in the lines italicized, 85 to 108, and a passage in Hooker's Ecclesiastical Polity, which I shall presently quote, has often been noted. That, and further resemblances not so frequently remarked between the tenor of Ulysses' argument as a whole and the teaching of Hooker in other parts of the Polity, we shall examine. But, to be fair, we should clear the field of borrowings or inspirations for which Shakespeare is indebted, certainly or presumably, to his acquaintance with other authors. We may then, setting Hooker's writing side by side with the residue, judge whether resemblances still persist.

The speech of Ulysses forms part of the heroic strand of Troilus and Cressida. For the dramatic impulse of the speech, its subject "the specialty of rule," and particularly for the phraseology of the first five lines (78–83) and the figure of the hive, Shakespeare is indebted to an English manipulation or translation of the second book of the Iliad—probably to Chapman's translation of 1598. From this also he seems to have derived the suggestion for the argument concerning "degree," and for the analogy between "the heavens themselves" with their shining dignitaries and the course of human governments. The analogy once suggested, Shakespeare remembers that there is an elaboration of the

same thought in the story from which he is drawing
the love-strand of his play, namely the Troilus and
Criseyde of Chaucer. To that passage in his Chaucer
he turns; and then perceiving that Chaucer, who
had translated the De Consolatione Philosophiae
of Boethius into prose, is paraphrasing from his own
translation, he naturally turns back to the translation as bound up in the same folio of Chaucer's
Works. From the figure, elaborated by both Boethius and Chaucer, of the harmony of the "country
of the stars," of the bond that holds the "elements"
of our earth and their "peoples joined in wholesome
alliaunce" under the governance of Love; from their
figure of the discord that would ensue if "Love
aught let his bridle go," we may be confident, if
one is ever justified in tracing the details of a poet's
fancy to a definite source, that Shakespeare drew
some of the details for the corresponding part of
the speech of Ulysses I should say, especially such
details as "the unity and married calm of states,"
line 100, and lines 111–113—

> The bounded waters
> Should lift their bosoms higher than the shores
> And make a sop of all this solid globe.

To be sure, with Boethius and Chaucer the bond
that holds the universe together is Love, whereas
with Shakespeare's Ulysses it is Law; but that does
not affect the underlying thought, for the "love"

of Boethius and Chaucer is also "law and wise judge to do equity." [1]

There is, however, much in the discourse of Ulysses that cannot be traced to materials in Chaucer, Boethius, and Homer, or to any contemporary treatment of the story. In none of these is the analogy between the political order and that of the celestial spheres developed as here; in none, the theory of government by supreme authority and degree. In none is the wreck of the planetary system described; and in none do we find the psychology of the discourse.

The doctrine of the harmonious order of the universe, sphere within sphere, is of course of the Pythagorean tradition, as handed down by Plato in the tenth book of the Republic, and as reduced to the geocentric system of astronomy by Ptolemy. The Ptolemaic system was still generally accepted in Shakespeare's time; and to such teaching may be attributed the poet's description of Sol as a planet whose sphere—or orbit—is midway between the others. As for the wreck of the universe, the fancy had been elaborated with jocose application by Rabelais, something of whose work was known to Shakespeare.[2] But from no such source does he derive the precise materials for the poetic analogy drawn by Ulysses of celestial and political law, still less the sequence of the discourse.

[1] For this indebtedness to Homer, Boethius, Chaucer, see Appendix E.

[2] See below, Appendix F.

The political philosophy resembles that with which writers of the Italian renaissance had familiarized Englishmen from the reign of Henry VII down. It is of Platonic-Aristotelian provenience and is plainly set forth in an educational treatise written by Sir Thomas Elyot in 1531. From chapters one and two of the first book of The Governour, Shakespeare could have derived hints for the political argument advanced by his Ulysses, for illustration, and even for phraseology. Elyot here touches upon the analogy of the heavenly spheres, emphasizes order, degree, and justice in governance, the "chaos" that ensues upon the disregard of them, and the destruction of the agent who brings about the dissolution; and he elaborates the economy of the bee. We must, however, remember that save the emphasis upon degree, there is little to Shakespeare's purpose in Elyot that Shakespeare had not already under his hand in Chaucer, Boethius, and the Iliad; that Elyot's is but one of the numerous expositions of the political doctrine accessible to the poet; and that the figures and phrases were the flotsam of conversation as well as of political literature in Shakespeare's day.[1]

Homer and Chaucer, surely,—Boethius, probably,—Elyot, possibly,—have suggested now one and now another phase of the thought, imagery, and diction, but in none are to be found the development of thought, the elaboration and application

[1] See Appendix G.

of imagery, the psychology which characterize the discourse of Ulysses as a whole. For these the most succinct and satisfactory contemporary parallelism is presented in a few closely sequent pages of Hooker's Ecclesiastical Polity. To the resemblance between the part about the celestial spheres and a paragraph in Hooker upon law, "as at once the rule of moral action and government, and the rule of moral agents," the Shakespearian editor, Verplanck, called attention some seventy years ago. "It is possible," says he, "that the poet had this thought suggested by an analogous passage, of equal eloquence, in his contemporary Hooker's Ecclesiastical Polity, of which the first parts were published in 1594. If it were not, it was no very strange coincidence between the thoughts of men of large and excursive minds, at once poetical and philosophical, applied to the most widely differing subjects."

The passage in the Ecclesiastical Polity (Bk. I, iii, 2) runs as follows: "God's commanding those things to be which are, and to be in such sort as they are, to keep that *tenure and course* which they do, importeth the establishment of nature's law. . . . And as it cometh to pass in a *kingdom rightly ordered*, that after a law is once published, it presently takes effect far and wide, all *states framing themselves thereunto*, even so let us think it fareth in the natural course of the world; since the time that God did first proclaim the edicts of his law upon it, *heaven and earth have hearkened unto his voice*, and their labour hath been to do his will: He 'made a law for the rain;' He gave his 'decree unto the sea, *that the waters should not pass his commandment.*' Now, *if nature should intermit her course,* and leave altogether though it were but for a while *the observation of her own laws;* if those principal and mother elements of the world, whereof all things in this lower world are made, should lose the qualities which now they have; *if the frame of that heavenly* arch erected over our heads should loosen and *dissolve itself; if celestial spheres should forget their wonted motions, and by irregular volubility turn themselves any way as it might happen; if the prince of the lights of heaven,* which now as a giant doth run his unwearied course, should as it were through a languishing faintness begin to stand and to rest himself; if the *moon should wander from her beaten way,* the times and *seasons* of the year blend themselves by *disordered and confused mixture, the winds breathe out their last gasp, the earth be defeated by heavenly influence,* the fruits of the earth pine away *as children at the withered breasts of their mother* no longer able to yield them relief: what would become of man himself, whom these things now do all serve? See we not plainly that *obedience of creatures unto the law of nature is the stay of the whole world?*" [1]

I have italicized for the convenience of the reader the more suggestive parallelisms in thought and

---

[1] Everyman edition, 156–7.

phrase between this passage and lines 85–98 of the speech of Ulysses.

We cannot but agree with Verplanck that in thought and eloquence Shakespeare is "singularly like" Hooker. The fact is, however, that both the Elizabethans had been reading Boethius De Consolatione, and that for both the initial suggestion of the figure of celestial harmony and discord proceeded from that author. Hooker, however, had used not the Chaucerian translation of Boethius but the original. In Book I, ii, 6, of the Polity,[1] just two pages before Hooker launches upon his poetic analogy, he quotes directly from Boethius the Latin introduction to the exposition of "the ordinance which moveth the heaven and the stars" and of the way in which, through Love, "the high thunderer . . . maketh interchangeable the perdurable courses;" and this Latin Hooker translates in terms not used by Chaucer.[2] In many other parts of the first book of the Polity Hooker's thought follows that of Boethius; and though both Hooker and Boethius make direct use of Aristotle's Ethics, in some instances it is evidently the language of Boethius and not of Aristotle that Hooker paraphrases. At first blush, therefore, one is inclined to explain the singular similarity between Shakespeare and Hooker in this spot by referring it altogether to the Boethian source. But upon further examina-

[1] Everyman edition, 153–4.
[2] See Appendix H.

tion it appears that, though the initial impulse to the employment of the celestial analogy is Boethian, the resemblance between Shakespeare and Hooker in the elaboration of it, in the description of the wreck of the universe, and in the subsequent discourse, cannot be explained in this way.

For his description of the wreck Hooker makes use of a source not consulted by Boethius and not known to Shakespeare, a Latin treatise of Arnobius, written about 303 A. D. And when we deduct from Shakespeare's development of the analogy as a whole the Chaucerian-Boethian parallelisms already noted, namely, "the bounded waters," "a sop of all this solid globe," etc., we find in what remains—"the heavens themselves, the planets, and this centre observe . . . insisture, course . . . season . . . in all line of order;" "in evil mixture to disorder wander;" "commotion in the winds," "what plagues and what portents," and various other items—a striking similarity with those sentences in Hooker which Hooker has almost literally translated from Arnobius.[1] Even though Shakespeare's brain might readily have furnished the words and phrases to his Ulysses, this continuance of similarity with Hooker alone justifies further pursuit of the investigation.

Verplanck, judging merely from what lay before him, is of the same opinion. "Hooker's subsequent remarks," he says, "singularly remind the reader of

[1] See Appendix H.

the more rapid view given by the poet of 'the unity and married calm of state' and the ills by which it is disturbed." Let us quote again "the more rapid view."

> Frights, changes, horrors
> Divert and crack, rend and deracinate
> 100 *The unity and married calm of states*
> Quite from their fixure! *O, when degree is shak'd,*
> *Which is the ladder to all high designs,*
> Then enterprise is sick! How could communities,
> Degrees in schools, and brotherhoods in cities,
> 105 *Peaceful commerce from dividable shores,*
> The primogenitive and due of birth,
> Prerogative of age, crowns, sceptres, laurels,
> *But by degree, stand in authentic place?*
> Take but degree away, *untune that string,*
> 110 And, hark, *what discord follows!*

The reader is already aware, as Verplanck was not, that "the unity and married calm of states" had its origin, almost its verbal expression, in Chaucer and Boethius. But Chaucer and Boethius say nothing about the destruction of "peaceful commerce" that follows upon the disturbance of unity and calm. Hooker and Shakespeare do.

In the paragraph already quoted from the Polity, when a "kingdom is rightly ordered . . . after a law is once published it presently takes effect far and wide, all states framing themselves thereunto." A few pages further on (I, x, 12–13) Hooker proceeds to the consideration of the Law of Nations—"which toucheth all such several bodies politic, *so far forth as one of them hath public commerce with another.*" We are not satisfied, says he, with the mutual participation of civil society, . . . "but we covet to have a kind of society and fellowship even with all mankind; . . . yea, to be in *league of amity with them:* and this not only *for traffick's sake,* or to the end that when many are confederated each may make the other more strong," but for knowledge sake. . . . But, as the laws of reason have not been "sufficient to direct each particular person in all his affairs and duties;" and, as the accessory "laws of polity and regiment . . . are not able now to serve, when men's iniquity is so hardly restrained within any tolerable bounds: in like manner, the *national laws of natural commerce* between societies of that former and better quality *might have been other than now, when nations are so prone to offer violence, injury and wrong.* . . . The strength and virtue of that law is such that no particular nation can lawfully prejudice the same by any their several laws and ordinances." [1]

If Shakespeare, in his substitution of "specialty of rule" and "degree" for the Chaucerian and Boethian Love, was in any way indebted to Hooker's exposition of natural law, to his imagery of the "celestial spheres" forgetting "their wonted motions," to his phraseology, of "tenure and course," order, "season," and for the striking detail of the wreck—which Hooker derives from Arnobius,—if

[1] Polity, 156, 198, 199.

he is indebted to Hooker for the exposition of laws
in the physical world, is it unlikely that he should
be impressed also by Hooker's exposition of law
in the social, political, and international world, and
so pass to illustration by detail in somewhat similar
strain? Let us take the steps in order and compare.

Hooker, in the lines following his imaginary wreck
of the universe, points the lesson not with a commonplace drawn from the Pythagorean and Platonic
harmony of the spheres, but with the figure of the
"untuned string:" "See we not plainly that *obedience of creatures unto the law of nature* is the stay of
the whole world? Notwithstanding with nature it
cometh sometimes to pass as with art . . . He
that striketh an instrument with skill *may cause
notwithstanding a very unpleasant sound,* if the string
whereon he striketh be uncapable of harmony." [1]
So, also, Shakespeare in lines 109–10, but substituting
degree among moral agents for obedience to the
law of nature: "Take but degree away, Untune that
string, And, hark, what discord follows."

Hooker proceeds immediately to the importance
of form, kind, order, degree in the fulfilment of law
not only by natural agents as "sociable parts united
into one body," but by voluntary as well—"Things
natural . . . observe their certain laws" when "they
keep those *forms* which give them their being . . .
seeing the *kinds* of their operations are both constantly and exactly framed according to the several

[1] Polity, 158.

ends for which they serve. . . . The natural generation [1] and process of all things receiveth *order
of proceeding* from the settled stability of divine
understanding. This appointeth unto them *their
kinds* of working. . . . That law, the performance
whereof we behold in things natural, is as it were an
authentical or an original draught in the bosom of
God himself." The second kind of law is of voluntary agents in societies. "Consider the angels of
God associated, and their law is that which disposeth them as an army, *one in order and degree
above another.*" So also with men, who are "next in
degree" to the angels, and "grow by degrees till
they come at length to be even as the angels themselves are" and who have their "laws politic, ordained for external order and regiment . . . unto
the common good for which societies are instituted."
Hooker then passes, as in the citation made above, to
the third kind of law as touching "all states," the
desire for "league of amity" between them, for
confederation of strength and for "traffick's sake,"
and to the baneful effect upon "national laws of
natural commerce" when "nations . . . offer violence, injury, and wrong." [2] In like manner but in
slightly altered sequence Shakespeare passes in

---

[1] The passage beginning "The natural generation" and ending "in the bosom of God himself" is a close paraphrase of
Boethius IV, Prose vi, 45–55; but not as translated by Chaucer;
nor did Chaucer take it over in his Troilus and Criseyde.

[2] Polity, 159, 160, 163, 164, 166, 188, 198.

lines 98 to 111 from the natural to the social: "The unity and married calm of states;" the deracination "from their fixure;" the shaking of degree "which is the ladder to all high designs;" "the communities" and "brotherhoods in cities," and "peaceful commerce from dividable shores," losing their "authentic place;" the untuned string, the discord.

Here again the resemblance may be accounted for as the result of natural procedure in logical and imaginative discourse, as pursued by men of the same literary atmosphere. But the joint evidence of similarity in general sequence and specific detail begins to assume a cumulative character pointing to more than coincidence.

Still other details call for consideration. In line 107, above—"Prerogative of age, crowns, sceptres"—would naturally occur to Ulysses; but I have frequently wondered why, in this enumeration of the disasters attending disregard of degree in its broader significance, Ulysses should have bothered his head—poetically, logically, or historically—about the fate of "degrees in schools." His creator may be pardoned for recollecting that there are such things as collegiate degrees; but the item seems far-fetched, and ridiculously specific. Is it mere coincidence that Hooker, too, speaks not only of collegiate communities and degrees, but of the prerogative of seniority and the sceptre of discipline? That toward the end of his Preface, only three sections before the illustration of the "kingdom rightly ordered,"

he should have said: "Therefore I wish that yourselves [Puritans objecting to permanent ranks
among ministers] did well consider how opposite
some of your positions are unto the state of collegiate
societies, whereon the two universities consist.
*Those degrees which their statutes bind them to take are
by your laws taken away.*" ? That he should have
made a special point of the inconvenience likely to
be entailed upon the "seniors" of those universities
by the abolition of collegiate orders? and that he
should have emphasized, at the end of the section,
the ticklish position of "*superiors* that will not have
the sceptre of discipline to rule over them;" and the
"perilous consequence . . . if the present state
of the highest governor placed over us, if the quality
and disposition of our nobles, if the orders and laws
of our famous universities" be upset?[1] If the resemblances already suggested between this speech
of Ulysses and the first book of the Polity are not a
mere matter of coincidence we must credit Shakespeare with the habit of reading the preface of a
book as well as the book itself.

At first glance the "singular" similarity to which
Verplanck has given us the clue seems to cease at
this point. In the continuation of the speech of
Ulysses, the first four lines find their immediate
motivation in Boethius and Chaucer—

110   Each thing meets
    In mere oppugnancy. The bounded waters

[1] Polity, 129, 130, 142.

Should lift their bosoms higher than the shores
And make a sop of all this solid globe.

"All that now loveth a-sonder sholde lepe" and the
sea should "drench earth," says Chaucer. "Alle
thinges that now loven hem to-gederes wolden
maken a bataile continuely," says Boethius; and
the sea would "streche his boundes up-on the erthes."
And the next five lines—

Strength should be lord of imbecility,
115 And the rude son should strike his father dead.
Force should be right; or rather right and wrong,
Between whose endless jar justice resides,
Should lose their names, and so should justice too.

may be an elaboration of the thought presented in
the same sources. "Amonges thise thinges sitteth
the heye maker, king and lord, . . . lawe and wys
juge, to don equitee," says Boethius.[1] But the
"right and wrong" no longer "judged rightly" by
"the faculty of reason," and "the Laws of well-
doing which are the dictates of Reason" are also
definitely emphasized in Hooker's sequence of discussion.

For the succeeding depiction of moral chaos, however, and for the psychology underlying, we find no
inspiration in Boethius and Chaucer. Ulysses
prognosticates:

Then everything includes itself in power,
120 Power into will, will into appetite;

[1] See Appendix E.

And appetite, an universal wolf,
So doubly seconded with will and power,
Must make perforce an universal prey,
And last eat up himself.

It has been suggested that for the thought not only
of the whole section (lines 114–124), but of the preceding—the disregard of "degrees in schools," and
"prerogative of age" the metaphor of musical discord—and of what follows about the "neglection of
degree. . . . That by a pace goes backward, in a
purpose It hath to climb," Shakespeare has had recourse to Plato's account in the Republic of the evils
of democracy and the tyranny that supervenes.
Some of the parallelisms in language as well as
thought are, indeed, not insignificant. The Republic, moreover, was accessible in Latin and French,
in continental disquisitions, and in an English exposition, in Shakespeare's time. Plato's theory of
democracy and its dangers was common property
through various English treatises as well, and had
become in political conversation a platitude. Simi-
larly accessible were his psychology—of appetite,
the spirited element, the reason. And so, too, was
Aristotle's restatement of it with the emphasis upon
will; and the ethics of both philosophers in which
justice appears as the harmonizer of faculties political
as well as individual.[1]

If, however, Shakespeare was deriving not merely

[1] See Appendix I.

from the material of every-day discourse, but from the printed page, no more accessible, comprehensive, or probable source for all this can be surmised than the first book of the Polity. The resemblance between the two writers in regard to ethics and psychology is no less striking than in the sequence and details already mentioned. Continuing the discussion of form, kind, order, degree among natural agents, angels and men, Hooker, who frequently cites Plato and Aristotle, says (I, vi, 5)—"Education and instruction are the means . . . *to make our natural faculty of reason both the better and the sooner able to judge rightly between truth and error, good and evil.* . . . It is in our *power,*" he continues, "to leave the things we do undone. . . . Choice there is not, unless the thing which we take be so in our power that we might have refused and left it. . . . To choose is *to will* one thing before another. And to will is to bend our souls to the having or doing of [i. e., the power over] that which they see to be good. Goodness is seen with the eye of the understanding. And the light of that eye is reason. So that two principal fountains there are of action, knowledge and will." Knowledge is of "good and evil" (right and wrong); *will* makes the "choice." "*Will* . . . differeth greatly from that inferior natural desire which we call *Appetite. The object of Appetite is whatsoever sensible good may be wished for; the object of Will is that good which Reason doth lead us to seek.* . . . *Appetite is the Will's solicitor, and the*

Will is Appetite's controller; . . . neither is any
other desire termed properly Will, but that where
Reason and Understanding, or the show of Reason,
prescribeth the thing desired." Where "*that good
which is sensible provoketh Appetite, and Appetite
causeth action, Reason being never called to counsel,* . . . *such actions are*" no longer "*to be counted
voluntary.* . . . Reason is the director of man's Will
by discovering in action [i. e., in the having or doing
that constitutes Power] what is good.   For the
Laws of well-doing are the dictates of Reason."   In
other words where reason is disregarded, law ceases
to exist; and where law, ruling through degree of
kind and function, as Hooker expounds, has ceased
to exist, the order of society is turned topsy-turvy.
For laws politic presume "*man to be in regard of his
depraved mind little better than a wild beast.*" [1]   This
is the "wolf" of Ulysses; and the climax reached by
Ulysses is that of Hooker: by progressive absorption—power swallowing everything, will swallowing
power, appetite swallowing will—all is included
"into appetite.   And appetite, an universal wolf. . . .
Must make perforce an universal prey, And last eat
up himself."

Let us now consider the resemblance in political
doctrine between Shakespeare and Hooker.   In the
closing lines of his discourse (124–137) Ulysses returns to the particular contention, the importance

[1] Polity, 168, 169, 170, 171, 188.

of degree in a government by law, the specialty of
rule with which he opened—

> Great Agamemnon,
> 125 This chaos, when degree is suffocate,
> Follows the choking; etc.

The classical doctrine of degree was no less material
of contemporary conversation for Shakespeare than
the ethics and psychology of which I have spoken.
But if Shakespeare had recourse to printed authority,
Hooker's page which is saturated with Aristotle,
as is Aristotle's with Plato, would answer his purpose as well as the originals or translations of them;
or as well as the writings of any by whom the doctrine had been popularized and applied to early
Christian, mediaeval, or modern conditions—St.
Augustine, St. Thomas Aquinas, Castiglione, Sir
Thomas Elyot. Better in fact, for Shakespeare's
conception of degree is not, like Plato's, Aristotle's,
the Italians', and Elyot's, based upon the tradition
of aristocratic caste, but, like that of Hooker, upon
merit and function.

Shakespeare does not, as some have thought, substitute degree—"the specialty of rule"—for law.
He conceives of law and degree precisely as does
Hooker. Law is the rule itself by which nature,
society and states are held in order. Degree is the
special instrumentality by means of which that rule
is made effective. "That which doth assign unto
each thing the kind, that which doth moderate the

force and power, that which doth appoint the form and measure, of working, the same we term a Law," says Hooker. "We term any kind of rule or canon, whereby actions are framed a law." [1] Degree, or "the specialty of rule," according to Hooker, is the series of "kinds" or "orders"—in nature, human society, and among the angels—to which law has assigned special functions for the harmonious fulfilment of its purpose. The series implies grades of relative superiority; but the function of each grade is relative to the capacity of the agents employed. And with Hooker, as we have seen, capacity of reason and of judgment develops with education. Degree, for Shakespeare as for Hooker, is that by means of which law distributes power and measure to the workings of nature and of society. Law rules the machine; degree is the series of cogs: the special instrumentality of rule. "Consider the angels," Hooker poetically exclaims, illustrating his doctrine of degree by the "corporation" of those who "have not disdained to profess themselves our 'fellow-servants:'" "Consider the angels associated, and their law is that which disposeth them as an army, one in order and degree above another." And, three pages further down, "Men, if we view them in their spring, are at the first without understanding or

---

[1] Polity, 150, 154: the pages immediately preceding those in which Shakespeare would find the analogy of the celestial spheres, employed by Ulysses in his exemplification of "the specialty of rule."

knowledge at all. Nevertheless from this utter vacuity they grow by degrees, till they come at length to be even as the angels themselves are." And, a little later: "To devise laws which all men shall be forced to obey none but wise men shall be admitted. Laws are matters of principal consequence; men of common capacity and but ordinary judgment are not able (for how should they?) to discern what things are fittest for each kind and state of regiment." In other words "degree" as with Shakespeare is "the specialty of rule," "the ladder to all high designs." It is not rule or law; nor on the other hand a series of social ranks in which, regardless of capacity, the position of the individual is fixed. In political society men "give their common consent all to be ordered by some whom they shall agree upon."[1]

When degree of due fitness and function under the law is suffocate, chaos, according to Shakespeare's Ulysses, "follows the choking:"

> And this neglection of degree is it
> That by a pace goes backward, in a purpose
> It hath to climb. The general's disdain'd
> 130   By him one step below, he by the next,
> That next by him beneath; so every step,
> Exampled by the first pace that is sick
> Of his superior, grows to an envious fever
> Of pale and bloodless emulation;

[1] Polity, 163, 166, 193, 190.

135   And 'tis this fever that keeps Troy on foot,
       Not her own sinews.

In similar tone Hooker, in the Preface to his book, admonishes Puritans who, objecting to orders and degrees in the Church of England and especially the requirement of license from a civil magistrate, abet the Barrowists in wrecking discipline: "The changes," says he, "likely to ensue through all states and vocations within this land, in case your desire should take place, must be thought upon." And in a passage which we have already quoted in part: "What other sequel can any wise man imagine *but this, that having first resolved that attempts for discipline without superiors are lawful, it will follow in the next place to be disputed what may be attempted against superiors which will not have the sceptre of that discipline to rule over them?*" [1] The sequel is that of Shakespeare's "neglection of degree."

I have said that the consentaneity of Shakespeare with Hooker is widely distributed through the works of the former. As regards the doctrine of degree, of aristodemocracy, of *noblesse oblige*, we have found it not only in Troilus and Cressida but in The Merchant of Venice (1594–6), All's Well that Ends Well (1595–1602), Henry V (1599), and in Sonnet 66 of about 1602. The repudiation of the divine right of kings appears in Richard II (1595–7), in other historical plays, and in Macbeth (1605–6); the distrust

[1] Polity, 128, 142.

of mob rule and flat democracy, in the historical plays again, in Julius Cæsar (1599–1600), Coriolanus (1609), and The Tempest (1611); equality before the law and the supremacy of justice in Richard II, Henry V, Measure for Measure (1603–4); justice in international affairs, in Henry V and Troilus and Cressida. The dignity of the individual and the rights of the poor are emphasized in many of the sonnets, in Hamlet (1602–4), in Lear (1604–6), and many other plays. From the citation of further parallels exemplifying the sympathy of Shakespeare with Hooker in respect of these and other phases of political and social theory I refrain lest I unduly repeat passages from one or the other already quoted in full.

I may, however, be pardoned, if I quote again those lines from Hamlet in which Shakespeare makes vocal the democratic murmur of his day, and call attention to a passage in Hooker. "For who," says the Prince of Denmark, subconsciously philosophizing,

> For who would bear the whips and scorns of time,
> The oppressor's wrong, the proud man's contumely,
> The pangs of disprized love, the law's delay,
> The insolence of office, and the spurns
> That patient merit of the unworthy takes. . .

For these lines, those who delight to trace Shakespeare to his sources have, so far as I know, found no parallel. Any such I venture to refer without prejudice or expression of opinion to Hooker, where in treating of laws and offices (I, x, 9), he says: "If the helm of chief government be in the hands of a few of the wealthiest, then laws providing for continuance thereof must make the punishment of contumely and wrong offered unto any of the common sort sharp and grievous, that so the evil may be prevented whereby the rich are most likely to bring themselves into hatred with the people, who are not wont to take so great offence when they are excluded from honours and offices as when their persons are contumeliously trodden upon."

So much concerning political consentaneity. The resemblances accumulate when we compare the views of poet and divine touching questions ethical and psychological. Though not precisely in the same language, still with similar eloquence of conviction Hooker, as well as Shakespeare, teaches that "there is some soul of goodness in things evil, Would men observingly distil it out;" that "there is nothing either good or bad, but thinking makes it so;" that "our virtues would be proud if our faults whipped them not; and our crimes would despair if they were not cherished by our virtues;" that "value dwells not in particular will;" that "no man is the lord of anything . . . Till he communicate his parts to others;" that man is "a beast no more—If the chief good and market of his time Be but to sleep and feed;" that by "discourse of reason" sound knowledge is attained, the will conducted, and the affections or forms of appetite controlled; that God "gave us not That capability and godlike reason To fust in us unused," though oftentimes the painfulness of knowledge or "some craven scruple of thinking too precisely on the event" may cause the will to shrink and decline the object that is good. No less eloquently than Hamlet has Hooker apostrophized man, noble in reason, infinite in faculties, "in form and moving how express and admirable! in action how like an angel! in apprehension how like a god! the beauty of the world! the paragon of animals!"

Parallels of this nature, though I am not unaware that masters from Plato to Montaigne had anticipated our two Elizabethans in the expression of one or another thought, I have relegated to an appendix for the benefit of those who may be curious.[1] But such readers I would remind that, in what is given there or what has already been quoted here, it is no part of my intent to prove deliberate dependence of the poet upon the divine. I am aiming merely to show that the Shakespeare who was acquainted with several of the founders of colonial liberty in America was also intimately acquainted with the philosophy which their wisest entertained; that he was not only sympathetic with their purposes but of like mind with the master to whom they were indebted for their political principles—the master from whom

[1] Appendix J.

our American forefathers consciously or unconsciously derived much that was essential to the erection of that "free popular state" whose "inhabitants should have no government putt upon them but by their own consente."

CHAPTER VIII

THE HERITAGE IN COMMON: ENGLAND, AMERICA, FRANCE

THE liberty we enjoy today is what it is, primarily because Southampton, Sandys and the Ferrars, Selden, Brooke, Coke, Sackville, Cavendish and other patriots were Englishmen; because Gates, De la Warr, and Strachey, Dale and Wyatt, the Bradfords, Brewsters, and Dudleys, willing to venture, were Englishmen; because in the decades when England was awakening to the perils of arbitrary rule at home, these contemporaries of Hooker and Shakespeare established in the New World an advance guard of English rights. From Shakespeare's England in an age when such civil and political rights were, with the possible exception of the United Netherlands, elsewhere unrealized, proceeded our common law, our trial by jury, our system of representative government, our free institutions. It is to Shakespeare's England that the Americans of the colonies owed—that Americans of today, of whatever stock they be, owe—the historic privileges that have made the New World a refuge for the oppressed and a hope for humanity. The sapling of civil liberty had drawn vigor from deep roots of

Anglo-Saxon, Anglo-Norman consciousness, and for centuries had strained steadily upward. In the seventeenth century it towered as an oak, and sheltered with its far-spread arms the Britons at home and Britons in America.

The thoughts that were common to Hooker and Shakespeare and Shakespeare's friends, the dream of the well-ordered state where merit shall govern, and not the favoritism of kings or their fabled divinity,—the ideals of individual worth, duty, and patriotism, were common to our English forefathers, the planters of Virginia, the pilgrims of the Mayflower and Plymouth, the puritans of Massachusetts Bay. *Caelum non animum mutant qui trans mare currunt.* The political instincts that, in the dawn of autocratic stress, were the heart and implicit moral of Shakespeare's histories and tragedies are the principles that pulsing into motive nerved the will and steeled the sinew of his younger contemporaries. The political freedom that, between 1609 and 1640, our English ancestors of Virginia and New England put into form and practice is the political freedom for which our grand-uncles of old England fought from 1642 to 1649, nay, to 1689. Bradford and Brewster, Winthrop and Endicott, John Cotton and Roger Williams, Harvard and Thomas Hooker, of New England, Alexander Whitaker, Clayborne, Bennett, and Nathaniel Bacon, of Virginia, belong to the history of English ideals no less than to that of America. And Hampden, Pym,

Cromwell, Milton and Bunyan, and the Seven
Bishops who defied the second James, were but
brothers to our English sires in New England.
Brothers of the same blood and ultimate ideal were
also the royalists of Virginia. Their conservatism
and devotion to a lost cause rendered them none
the less certain "in the free air of the New World
to develop into uncompromising democrats and
fierce defenders of their own privileges."

I

Of all these Englishmen of the seventeenth century, whether of the Old World or the New, there
was a heritage in common. One language welded of
the Old English, Scandinavian, Gallic and Latin:
manly, direct, sober and natively consistent; un-
fettered, experimental, acquisitive; from emergency
to emergency shaped according to the need, incomparable in riches ever cumulative. One race, one
nation, one blood infused of many strains and diverse
characteristics: of the Anglo-Saxon, the personal
independence and native conservatism; of the Nor-
man, the martial genius, equity, political vision,
masterful and unifying authority,—and of the Nor-
man, the chivalry, the romance and culture, too;
of the Celt, intermingling with these in the centuries
that flowed into Shakespeare, a current of aspira-
tion, poignant passion, poetic imagination—stirring
the blood but not intoxicating the Anglo-Norman

reason. One custom, of spiritual ideal but of tried experience—practical rather than speculative, distrustful of veering sentiment, slowly crystallizing into the stability of a national consciousness: a custom of individual prerogative and of obedience to the authority that conserves the prerogative; of fair play and equality of opportunity, of fearless speech for the right, and simple for the common weal; a custom making for popular sovereignty, for allegiance, for national honor in national fair dealing, for the might that is right; one custom, mother of the law. One common law: the progressive expression "of a free people's needs and standards of justice;" the outgrowth of social conditions, deriving its authority not from enactment of sovereign monarch or sovereign legislature but from the aggregate social will—the law of precedent and of the righteous independence of the courts.

Long before Magna Charta features of this law, this conservatively expanding charter of liberties and duties, are distinguishable in the procedure of our forefathers in England. From the days of Ethelbert to those of Alfred, and from Alfred to Edward the Confessor, for four and a half centuries before the Conquest this law, hardly if at all affected by foreign corpus or code, had been "gathering itself together out of the custom of" the independently developing Anglo-Saxon. This sanction "the Conqueror, who claimed the crown by virtue of English law and professed to rule by English law," repeatedly bound himself to observe, "and he handed down the tradition to all who came after him." [1] This law of national precedent, further developed under Henry II and systematically expounded by Glanvil, or by some clerk under his direction, grew into the Great Charter of King John with its equal distribution of civil rights to all classes of freemen, and its restriction of monarchical prerogative. "The king," writes Bracton in the days of John's successor, Henry III, "must not be subject to any man but to God and the law; for the law makes him king. Let the king therefore give to the law what the law gives to him, dominion and power; for there is no king where will, and not law, bears rule." [2] The relation of this English law of custom to the general nature of law as set forth in the civil code of the Roman system, Bracton expounds; but from that system the peculiar English law is not derived. Expanding through Fortescue and Littleton this English law is the common law of Coke; and by the Virginia charter of 1606, probably drafted by Coke, the rights of the common law were conferred upon the colonists of the New World.

For these Englishmen of the "sceptred isle" and of the untilled wilderness of the west there had been one spirit energizing toward freedom—civil and religious; one charter of rights and obligations. Of political development there had been a continuous

---

[1] Freeman, Comparative Politics, p. 114.
[2] The Laws and Customs of England, Bk. I, ch. viii.

history for eleven hundred years before England was planted in America. There had also been one literature, as ancient and as noble, stirring in embers of racial tradition—a tradition of service and heroism and generous acceptance of fate; kindling to mirth and pity, humanity and reverence; leaping to flame in imagination and power; and, in the decades when first the English peopled "worlds in the yet unformèd Occident," attaining full glory in the zenith of Shakespeare.

Not with those eleven hundred years ceased the oneness of the English heritage. For a period longer than that which has elapsed since the American branch of the Anglo-Saxon race has been a separate nation, the heritage was one. One hundred and forty years have succeeded our declaration of independence. Through the hundred and seventy which preceded, the history of Britain was the continuing property of our forefathers of Virginia and New England. Not only Hampden and Cromwell and the Ironsides, but Chatham, Holland, Burke, and Sir Philip Francis, were compatriots of the colonials. The admirals of the fleet, Blake, Vernon, Anson, Hawke, were our admirals. It was for the nascent empire of our British and British-American forefathers that they won the supremacy of the sea. The victories of Marlborough, Clive's conquest of India, Wolfe's conquest of Canada—to which the young George Washington contributed the services of his still British sword—were glories

not of a foreign race but of our race. For four generations we have been an independent people. But
for six generations before that the intellectual and
spiritual strivings of our British compatriots toward
truth and freedom were those of the British in
America. Harrington, Algernon Sidney, Locke,
Hume and Berkeley were ours. And in literature,
Milton and Bunyan, Dryden and Pope, Swift,
Addison, Gray and Goldsmith were our poets and
essayists. Such was the birthright of our British
forefathers in the American colonies. True it is, that
in legal procedure they preferred, during the years
of primitive social conditions, the appeal to divine
law and the law of reason or of human nature, as
expounded by Hooker and his school, to any kind of
law positive; and it is true that, within the field of
positive law, they took more kindly to the civil
which derives authority from enactment than to the
common which derives from precedent. But when
they reached "the stage of social organization which
the common law expressed," they were only too glad
to claim that birthright also, as conveyed by various
early charters.[1] And upon such right they based
their appeal for civil liberty.

Not at all with 1776 did the English heritage cease
to be the same for the sons of England at home and
over the seas. In their resistance to taxation without

[1] Nathan Abbott, Characteristics of the Common Law, in
St. Louis Congress, Vol. II, 283—from Dr. Reinsch, Bulletin
Univ. Wisconsin, no. 31.

representation, to coercion by force, to the Acts of Trade, the colonists in America were supported by Fox and the elder Pitt, by Shelburne, Camden, Burke, Rockingham, and all true patriots at home. Americans were asserting their rights as Englishmen under charter and common law. "Do not break their charter; do not take away rights granted them by the predecessors of the Crown!" cried members of the English House of Commons. Pitt "pointed out distinctly that the Americans were upholding those eternal principles of political justice which should be to all Englishmen most dear, and that a victory over the colonies would be of ill omen for English liberty, whether in the Old World or the New." Speaking of the tea-duty Lord North had asseverated, "I will never think of repealing it until I see America prostrate at my feet." To this Colonel Barré retorted, "Does any friend of his country really wish to see America thus humbled? In such a situation she would serve only as a monument of your arrogance and your folly. For my part the America I wish to see is America increasing and prosperous, raising her head in graceful dignity, with freedom and firmness asserting her rights at your bar, vindicating her liberties, pleading her services, and conscious of her merit. This is the America that will have spirit to fight your battles, to sustain you when hard pushed by some prevailing foe. . . . Unless you repeal this law you run the risk of losing America." In the House of Lords, three devoted defenders of American liberty were the Dukes of Portland, Devonshire and Northumberland. They were descended from Henry Wriothesley, third earl of Southampton, the founder with Sir Edwin Sandys of the charter liberties of Virginia.[1] In that House, protesting against the "Intolerable Acts" of 1774, the Duke of Richmond thundered, "I wish from the bottom of my heart that the Americans may resist, and get the better of the forces sent against them." Not the historical precedent of England or the political wisdom of her best "arrayed her in hostility to every principle of public justice which Englishmen had from time immemorial held sacred," but the perversity of an un-English prince and of his fatuous advisers. Bent upon thwarting the policy of reformers who would make the Commons more truly representative of the English people, upon destroying the system of cabinet government, and resuscitating the theory of divine right, these unfortunates picked their quarrel with the American colonies. "For," as John Fiske shrewdly remarks, "if the American position that there should be no taxation without representation, were once granted, then it would straightway become necessary to admit the principles of parliamentary reform," and to call the liberals to power in England. A representation of the colonies in Westminster, though favored by some great Englishmen, might have been impracticable; but if George III had listened to the elder

[1] Brown, Eng. Pol. in Va., 147.

Pitt and his followers, he would have recognized the right of American freemen to levy their own taxes, and the revolution would have been obviated. The would-be autocrat forced the issue in America and was defeated. If there had been no revolution in America there would have been a revolution in England, and the monarch would in all probability have been dethroned. The War of Independence reasserted for England as well as for America the political rights for which Englishmen, from the time of King John to that of James I, from the time of Hooker, Shakespeare, Sandys, Bradford, Winthrop. Sir Thomas Dale and Sir Francis Wyatt, to that of Cromwell, had contended. It confirmed the victories of the Great Rebellion and of the Revolution of 1688. The younger Pitt denounced the war against the American colonies as "most accursed, wicked, barbarous, cruel, unnatural, unjust, and diabolical." And when Charles Fox heard that Cornwallis had surrendered at Yorktown, he leaped from his chair and clapped his hands.[1] The victory at Yorktown dissipated once for all the fatal delusion of divine prerogative. Those who conceived and carried through the American Revolution were Anglo-Saxons: Otis, Samuel and John Adams, Hancock, Henry, Richard Henry Lee, Franklin, Jefferson, Washington. The greatest of Americans was the greatest Englishman of his age: Washington was but asserting against

[1] See John Fiske, The American Revolution, I, 26, 34, 35, 40, 42, 45, 62, 93, 98, 100; II, 286.

a despotic sovereign of German blood and broken English speech the prerogative of the Anglo-Saxon breed, the faith of his liberal brothers in England.

Political history has, indeed, worn its independent channel; but spirit and speech, letters, order of freedom and control in the America of today are of the ancient blood and custom.

Our Monroe doctrine is as old as Shakespeare's day: it is but Sir Edwin Sandys's "Where no government shall be putte upon them save by their own consente," adapted to the conditions of a new continent. Our zeal for arbitration is but Hooker's desire for "an universal fellowship with all men." For our doctrine of the "freedom of the seas," England has consistently contended, and has been defeated of her aim, only because the central autocracy of Europe has refused to concede a like "freedom of the land." Conspicuously ours, conspicuously theirs of modern England, as in the day of Hooker and Sandys, Selden and Coke, when it first attained full consciousness, is that which lies at the heart of all Shakespeare's utterance regarding individual prerogative—the due process of law: the law of precedent and fair play and righteous independence of the courts. "A great element of civil liberty" is this, wrote an eminent German jurist before the present German War, "and part of a real government of law which in its totality has been developed by the Anglican tribe alone." It was in the English Inns of Court that Winthrop, Bellingham, and

Dudley gained the rudiments of that common law; there, too, the Virginian leaders of bench and bar at the planting of the colony, and in her palmiest days; there, too, many of the signers of the Declaration of Independence. From the Atlantic to the Pacific this system of law "better suited to the needs of a free people and an advancing civilization than the civil, which obtained its historical form under an absolute empire," has been established by those who have inherited the institutions of the England of the early seventeenth century. And still, three hundred years after our founding, "the resemblances between the common law in America and its parent in England are greater than the differences, and the differences are rather in degree than in kind."[1] America still holds to the wisdom of her Shakespearian ancestors.

II

Much as we owe to monarchical France for her assistance during our War of Independence against her English rival for European and colonial supremacy; much as we cherish the long-continued and unselfish amity of republican France, and similar as her devotion and ours to the creed of equal human dignity and equal intellectual opportunity; sym-

[1] E. McClain, History of Law, 270; and Nathan Abbott, Characteristics of the Common Law, 274, 283, in St. Louis Congress, Vol. II.

pathetic as we are in democratic polity and ideal; and indissoluble as the bond with her in the sisterhood of free powers,—to say, as does a recent writer in one of our most dignified and authoritative American periodicals, that "it was from the philosophers of the French Revolution that we learned the ideals of equal citizenship and republicanism," [1] is not only to invert the sequence of history but to misstate a fundamental issue. To assert that "the ideas of Rousseau, much more than the political theories of the mother country, inspired us in our first efforts toward democratic liberty," is to distort our relation with the one country from which we derive our political traditions, aspirations, and free institutions. The authors of our Declaration of Independence inherited not from Rousseau or any French philosopher but from their own ancestors and cousins, the liberal statesmen and political philosophers of England; and from their own colonial ancestors, by whom the principles of Anglo-American political theory had been developed before 1776 in the experience of the various colonial governments. The philosophers of the French Revolution learned the ideals of equal citizenship and republicanism from England; and the leaders of that revolution were inspired by the English Revolution of 1688 and the American of 1776. "There is no evidence to show that Rousseau's Contrat Social of 1762 was a force" at the time of the Declaration of Independ-

[1] Arthur Bullard, Atlantic Monthly, Nov., 1916, pp. 635–636.

ence; "and the doctrines ascribed to him were really those of Locke, who was the quarry from whom the Revolutionary fathers drew both thoughts and phrases." [1] "There is abundant evidence of the fact that Locke's Essays on Government were read and studied in the Revolutionary period." [2] Locke is continually quoted as final authority in their discussions and writings. "Locke was the philosopher of the American Revolution, as he was of the Revolution of 1688." [3] And since Locke was a student of Hooker, here again we go back to the germinating thought of Shakespeare's day.

For Locke, the compact by which man passes out of a state of nature and governments come into existence has two stages. First, the formation of a society, or commonwealth, each individual agreeing to surrender to it, not all his natural rights to life, liberty, and estate, but his single right of executing the law of nature and punishing offenses against that law. This agreement is perpetual and irrevocable. Second, the formation of institutions for the government of the commonwealth. By agreement with a dynasty or king or other ruler—monarchical, oligarchical or democratic—the commonwealth places authority in the hands of a government for the attainment of the ends of civil and political society.

[1] A. B. Hart, National Ideals, p. 98.
[2] A. C. McLaughlin, Social Compact, etc., in Am. Hist. Rev., V, 467, 468.
[3] *Ibid.*

This is a contract between the commonwealth (constituted by the social pact) and the ruler; and it is subject to revision by the commonwealth whenever organic change is necessitated for the common good. If the ruler override his prerogative, the contract is broken and the commonwealth absolved from its allegiance. Not the ruler is supreme, but the legislative power; and even it is not absolute, but limited by fundamental and known laws.[1] This was the doctrine by which our forefathers justified their revolt. Of course Locke knew that the state of nature was an assumption, and the social compact a fiction. But he was himself unable to disprove them and they served his purpose: to justify the Revolution of 1688.

According to Rousseau, on the other hand, by an original contract of society, which people emerging from a state of nature ought to have signed—but did not, the people would become sovereign. There should be no second stage, no contract between the people and a government, whether of king or any other ruler. The sovereign power of the people is "inalienable, indivisible, and it would seem, infallible, if you can only get the 'general will' truly expressed." The executive and judicial powers may be entrusted to agents who are creatures of the sovereign people. But the legislative power, which

[1] Frederick Pollock, History of the Science of Politics, pp. 29–31; Wm. A. Dunning, The Political Philosophy of John Locke, in Political Science Quarterly, XX, 232–233.

is absolute, cannot be delegated to representatives. It must remain in the hands of the people and be exercised by them alone. Since the people of any but a small country are too numerous to get together and legislate it is hard to see how in Rousseau's democracy they would be any better off than they were in a state of nature. And if such despots delegate their legislative sovereignty to chosen representatives—as Rousseau's disciples did—they but set up a Frankenstein in comparison with whose delegated despotism the state of nature would be paradise. Rousseau assumes conditions different from those which confronted our forefathers of 1776, and he develops his theory in a way that Locke would have considered subversive of all constitutional government.

Locke was advocating a delegated and limited sovereignty in the hands of aristodemocracy; Rousseau, "a democracy of the extremest type" whose sovereignty was absolute, and whose law-making power in the hands of all, no matter how ignorant. With Locke "the contract was made mainly to protect property." With Rousseau, the same; but he "places property at the discretion of the sovereign people"—a doctrine which, though later retracted by him, was and *is* the basis of the wildest communism. Thus Rousseau developed the doctrines of Locke, the thinkers of the Protectorate, and Hooker before them, into "the destructive democracy and direct sovereignty of the people" *which* manifested themselves in the excesses of 1789 to 1793.[1] But if these English philosophers had not enunciated their premises, Rousseau's Contrat Social would never have been evolved. For Rousseau was a careful student of Locke; and in Locke there is little that was not derived from the immediately preceding political philosophy of England. It was also from the writers of the English Revolution of 1689, especially Locke, and from observation of English constitutional government, that the philosophers of the French Revolution other than Rousseau derived most of the essentials of their democratic theory.[2]

Rousseau's influence upon the America of 1776 was practically *nil*. It pertains rather to the period succeeding 1789. The idea of government as the creature of the sovereign people, with its various corollaries, is "much more in harmony with later American conditions [from 1830 on] than was the idea of Locke;" but the fact remains that "the American Revolution was fought out on the principle of the English philosopher and in recognition of the idea of a contract between king and people. . . . And the notion was too firmly rooted not to retain its hold long after the adoption of the Constitution."[3]

In the Constitution itself, and in the classical

[1] W. Graham, English Political Philosophy from Hobbes to Maine, 56, 59, 66–7, 69.

[2] Gooch, Hist. Eng. Democratic Ideas, 357–8.

[3] McLaughlin, Social Compact, etc., 479.

contemporaneous commentary on and in defense of it, the Federalist, there is indeed manifest the authority of Montesquieu's treatise on The Spirit of Laws, 1748; but "of the supposed influence of other continental authors such as Rousseau there are few direct traces in the Federal Constitution." With Montesquieu's doctrine of the separation of powers in the three coördinate departments of government our fathers were thoroughly acquainted. But it was from England that Montesquieu derived the doctrine: the England of Magna Charta, the Petition of Right, the Bill of Rights. "Contrasting the private as well as public liberties of Englishmen with the despotism of Continental Europe Montesquieu had taken the Constitution of England as his model system, and had ascribed its merits to the division of legislative, executive, and judicial functions which he discovered in it, and to the system of checks and balances whereby its equilibrium seemed to be preserved." [1] Both the doctrine and the safeguard were, however, developed by Blackstone as well, whose Commentaries of 1765 were in the hands of all American publicists. And, so far as the separation of the legislative and executive powers is concerned, the doctrine had already been expounded by Locke,[2] of whom Montesquieu and Blackstone were students. As to the independence of the judicial power in case of conflict between the

[1] Bryce, American Commonwealth, I, 29.
[2] Of Civil Government, Secs. 143–159.

law-making power and the executive, or of oppression of the people by either, that is again and again implied by Locke. "The legislative, or supreme authority, . . . is bound to dispense justice, and decide the rights of the subject by promulgating standing laws, and known authorized judges." "Those who are united into one body, and have a common established law and judicature to appeal to, with authority to decide controversies between them, and punish offenders, are in civil society with one another." Though he subsumes under the legislative both the law-making and the judicial functions, he emphasizes always the independence of the "judges with authority to appeal to." [1]   What Montesquieu did was to clarify and systematize Locke's suggestion; and in the background of Locke's consciousness was always Hooker's Ecclesiastical Polity.

Whatever influence the French philosophers had upon the course of American political theory and practice was in general an influence derived by France from England, and the major part of any such influence belongs, as we have seen, to the years succeeding 1789. What the framers of our Constitution did not owe to the initiative of English political and legal writers, they owed to their own experience of the English common law, to "the experience of their colonial and state governments, and especially, for this was freshest and most in point, the experience of the working of the State Constitu-

[1] Civ. Gov., Secs. 136, 87, and 20, 21, 88, 240, 241.

tions, framed at or since the date when the colonies threw off their English allegiance. . . . The American Constitution is no exception to the rule that everything which has power to win the obedience and respect of men must have its roots deep in the past, and that the more slowly every institution has grown, so much the more enduring is it likely to prove. . . . Whatever success it has attained must be in large measure ascribed to the political genius, ripened by long experience, of the Anglo-American race. . . . There is little in this Constitution that is absolutely new. There is much that is as old as Magna Charta." [1]

Neither the American appeal to the natural rights of man and the social compact, nor the doctrine of the separation of governmental powers, was borrowed from France. Nor was the idea of a federal union. That owes nothing to the experience of any Continental country: not to the leagues of ancient Greece; not to the modern Swiss cantons or the United Netherlands. It was the application of the "compact" philosophy of Locke to the exigency of American conditions at the American moment. "No one who has studied the primary material will be ready to assert that" the framers of the Constitution "consistently and invariably acted upon a single principle, that they were altogether conscious of the nature and import of what was being done, and that they constantly spoke with logical ac-

[1] Bryce, Am. Com. I, 28–30.

curacy of the process. . . . But as far as one can find a consistent principle, it is this, that by compact of the most solemn and original kind a new political organization and a new indissoluble unit was being reared in America. The compact was sometimes spoken of as a compact between the individuals of America in their most original and primary character," constructing society anew; "sometimes it was looked on as a compact between groups of individuals," or States, "each group surrendering a portion of its self-control and forming a new order or unity just as society itself was constituted." [1] Here again not only does the "compact" theory come from Locke, but the hint of federal organization. For with the legislative and executive branches of government he coördinates also what he calls the "federative." And his remarks concerning the federative function of government—"the power of war and peace, leagues and alliances, and all the transactions with all persons and communities without the Commonwealth"—are no less applicable to the inter-state relations of sovereign commonwealths or groups, entering the "more perfect Union," than to the relations of the more perfect Union, or federal Commonwealth in its totality, with foreign persons and communities.[2]

Far from being true that from the philosophers of the French Revolution "we learned the ideals of

[1] McLaughlin, Social Compact, etc., 472.
[2] Of Civil Government, Secs. 146–148.

citizenship and republicanism," and that "the ideas of Rousseau much more than the political theories of the mother country inspired us in our first efforts toward democratic liberty," not only we but the French themselves learned the political theories—legal equality, sovereignty of the people, participation in government—and derived the inspiration of democratic liberty from English philosophers and from English and Anglo-American experience. It was Locke's theory, based, I repeat, upon that of Hooker and of his disciples, the founders of our first American charters of freedom; it was Locke's theory of the transformation of a state of nature into a civil state by a contract; Locke's theory of legal and political equality and of "a sovereignty of the people without too much of either sovereignty or people; . . . of natural rights, but not too many of them, and of a separation of powers that was not too much of a separation;" Locke's theory of the right of resistance and the "appeal to Heaven,—" that justified the English Revolution of 1688 and the Bill of Rights, and vivified the succeeding constitutional reforms. Locke's theory "was brought over, supported by the practical illustration of the accomplished English Revolution, to the Continent, where many of its elements were taken up and developed to their logical limits" and beyond by [Rousseau and other] thinkers of France." [1] It was this same theory,

[1] Wm. A. Dunning, The Political Philosophy of John Locke, Pol. Sci. Quart., XX, 245.

as embodied in the American Declaration of Rights of 1774, and in that of Independence, and successfully asserted by our Revolution, and more or less reflected in our Anglo-American Constitution, that inspired the thinking patriots of the French Revolution. It was the same theory, tinctured with dangerous elaborations from Rousseau, that in 1789 inspired the French Declaration of the Rights of Man. "Celebrated writers of France and England," says Jefferson, who was our minister plenipotentiary in Paris at the time, "had already sketched good principles on the subject of government; yet the American Revolution seems first to have awakened the thinking part of the French nation in general from the sleep of despotism in which they were sunk. The officers too, who had been to America, were mostly young men, less shackled by habit and prejudice, and more ready to assent to the suggestions of common sense, and feelings of common rights, than others. They came back with new ideas and impressions. The press, notwithstanding its shackles, began to disseminate them; conversation assumed new freedoms; politics became the theme of all societies, male and female, and a very extensive and zealous party was formed, which acquired the appellation of the Patriotic party, who, sensible of the abusive government under which they lived, sighed for occasions of reforming it." And again, "The appeal to the rights of man, which had been made in the United States, was taken up by France, first of the European nations. So inscrutable is the arrangement of causes and consequences in this world, that a two-penny duty on tea, unjustly imposed in a sequestered part of it, changes the condition of all its inhabitants." It was France, then a despotism, that lent us Lafayette, and Rochambeau and his six thousand Frenchmen, "to deal England a blow where she would feel it"—a loan ineffaceable from American memory. It was Lafayette, returning to France, imbued with the spirit of American liberty, who in 1789, prepared, and proposed to the National Assembly, the Declaration of the Rights of Man. As a republic France is the younger sister of America.

Of the triad of modern democracies, not only the French Republic but the union of free commonwealths, styled the British Empire, is, in order of historical realization, a younger sister of the United States of America. But the nursing mother of all three democracies was the liberal England of the seventeenth century, liberalism at death grips with the autocratic Stuarts. During the last ten years of the preceding century that liberalism, long conceived, had at last found constructive philosophical expression in the teachings of Richard Hooker. In Shakespeare it spoke as poetry; in Southampton and Sandys and the early colonists, as practical experiment. It was legally defended by Coke and Selden. By the popular revolts of that century, it achieved political acceptance. In the writings of Milton, Harrington, Algernon Sidney, and Locke.

it was re-created for new and greater effort. In the century that followed, that liberalism, embodied in the New Whigs at home and in the patriots of the American Revolution, set America free, assured free government for Great Britain and laid the foundations of a saner colonial and territorial polity for the future. Without the aid of the noble Frenchmen—Beaumarchais, Lafayette, Rochambeau, St. Simon, de Grasse, America might not have gained her independence. The liberalism of those men, and of the French philosophers of political reform, was of mingled efflorescence; but the seed was in the liberalism of Hooker, of his disciples, Shakespeare's friends, and of Shakespeare himself. It flamed into first bloom with the Great Rebellion and the Commonwealth; into second, with the English Revolution and with Locke. By precept and example alike English liberalism, in the closing years of the eighteenth century, fired the leaders of the French Revolution and pointed the path for the French Republic of the present day.

CHAPTER IX

THE MEANING FOR US TODAY

SINCE the two-penny duty on tea and the shot heard round the world from Concord, a hundred and forty years have passed; and again inscrutable is the arrangement of causes and consequences in the history of freedom. An assassin's bullet at Serajevo furnishes the military despotisms of Central Europe with a pretext to unleash east, west, and south, the hounds of territorial conquest and tyrannic lust. All proposals for conference are rejected by the Central Powers. Serbia, appealing to the bar of nations, is attacked by Austria abetted by Germany. Russia, neither desirous of war nor ready for it, still hoping for a peaceful settlement mobilizes to fulfil her treaty obligations by a powerless protégé, and is countered by Germany armed to the teeth and fulminating ultimatums at just the moment when her ally is disposed to conciliation. The carnage is let loose. That democratic France may be bled to the white, the solemn stipulations of international law and the sanctions of humanity are cast to the winds by the Central Powers; and Germany as an incident tramples Belgium, "the suffering servant of the great community of mankind," raped, mutilated, murdered, into the blood-stained earth. Britain, mindful of her pledges, her democratic faith, her duty to the larger liberty, springs to arms. The conflict involves Europe, Asia, Africa—the dominions in both hemispheres. To the powers of ruthless and unbridled might, now drunk with blood, the conventions of belligerents, the safeguards of noncombatants, the privileges of neutrals, are as nothing. Hell belches its poisonous gases and liquid fire. The flag of truce is desecrated; physicians abandon their wounded prisoners to the onslaught of infectious disease. The dying and the ministrants of the cross are marked for slaughter. Death, for no conceivable military advantage, is rained upon country-side, hamlet, unfortified town. Peasants and artisans—old men and women, helpless youths and maidens—are shot in squads or deported into slavery worse than death. Conspiracies are launched against peoples at peace and in amity. Hospital ships, neutral ships, American ships, noncombatant ships, unarmed and unwarned, are wantonly destroyed. Mother and babe and sister of mercy sink; the cry of the drowning is mocked. Terror walks the earth. Brutality rules the waves.

Inscrutable indeed is the arrangement of causes and consequences in this world. A shot is fired in Bosnia; and the exultant autocracies wreck civilization. America protesting is flouted and attacked, driven to defend herself,—and accorded, at last, her chance to repay some fraction of the debt long due to France, her justification to rescue for England, to consecrate anew for herself, the Anglo-Saxon heritage. Questioning long, tried to the verge of patience and of honor, calmly deliberating, without rancor, or thought of personal gain other than the preservation of her independence and international prerogative, she ranges herself. Dignified and powerful beyond all dream of her English lovers and champions of 1769, America "with freedom and firmness, asserts her rights and vindicates her liberties"—not "at the bar of England," as that grand old colonel of the eighteenth century House of Commons had dreamed, nor of any earthly Power; not for herself alone but for mankind, at the bar of universal justice. With England and France and the free peoples of the world she has "the spirit to fight the battle," to sustain for posterity the cause of righteousness, peace, democracy, "hard pressed by a prevailing foe."

The humanism of Shakespeare and Hooker and the founders of colonial liberty in America, the humanism of their colonial successors and of the Revolutionary perpetuators of Anglo-Saxon liberty, called for the well-rounded man. It called for the man of intellect and vigor, emotionalized, and issuing in freedom,—in character with its moral implications, standards, and responsibilities. It called for the character that should promote the humanities of life. The intellectual arrogance that distinguishes the prevailing foe today found no place in Shakespeare's microcosm of human worth; nor has it found acceptance in Shakespeare's England or in any modern democracy, monarchical or republican, of civilized ideals. Civilized ideals are not skin-deep. Civilization is not a creature of self-interest or a vizard to force. It cannot be called into existence by a hundred and fifty years of highly specialized education, by inculcation of a goose-step, authority of a sabre, contempt of the poor in spirit and pure of heart. Civilization is born of personal dignity and human sympathy. It is ingrained by centuries of kindly manners and consideration of the other and the weak. Its ideals are not assumed: they are the breath of its nostrils, the vision of its heart; they fill the spaces of the soul. The ideals of the prevailing foe today are those of their forbears, the Teutonic Knights of the Middle Ages who, "converting" the pagans of Prussia, despoiled them of honor and property, and bequeathed to them the heritage of morals and manners by which they are known among nations today. The ideals of the Teutonic Knights are realized anew in Northern France and Belgium, Serbia and Poland, in the year of grace, 1917.

The cult of the acquisitive intellect whether for the enforcement of a civilization in veneer or for the development of technical, professional, commercial, or political efficiency, cannot but abase the conscience and heart: cannot but entail the overlordship of power, with cunning as its satellite. The worship of mere intellect is absolutely repugnant to the Anglo-American conception of manhood—of truth, right, and fellow-feeling, commingled for the good of the individual and of society. Out of relation to these, mentality becomes illogical, goes insane, perpetrates crime disgusting, unspeakable, attains its climax in suicide.

Shakespeare and the founders of our liberty regarded with reprobation the Machiavellianism of their day, that the end justifies the means: the end —the pagan glory of the state, nay of the Prince; the means—the exaltation of the expedient over the right. With like reprobation, they would, if living now, regard a dynastic philosophy by which in a certain quarter of the globe intellect has been fostered as intellect-for-greed, and federalized as intellect-for-power, to the suppression of individual liberty in action and opinion, the suppression of the individual moral code, the suppression of spontaneous and enlightened sympathy, and of a self-ordered and self-governing national conscience. In the Anglo-American consciousness there can be found no condonation for a state-craft by which intellect-for-power has been apotheosized; for an educational priest-craft by which war has been ritualized as the highest activity of the state; no palliation for national servility to the right of the state alone—to a right divine of a state that is law unto itself, and therefore above Law. Where the sophistry of intellect deploys in a void, its expediency, its "Necessity," is self-evoked and self-created. When that state wrecks "the married calm of states," every instrument of success becomes a legitimate weapon, and the frightfulness of modern scientific ingenuity deploys in the flesh. Where there is no divinity but that of the coterie, oligarchy or dynastic house, that calls itself the state, there is no divinity of universal justice and universal grace, and therefore no humanity. In such a nation, there is developed a condition of political psychology incomprehensible to the rest of mankind. Its Necessity justifies a deliberate reversion to barbarism, a carnival of blood and lies, a sniveling hypocrisy that would fail to hoodwink the veriest imbecile in any of God's asylums of the free. That such subterfuge should convince those who have inherited the ill-gotten gains of Frederick II and of Bismarck does not surprise. That it should delude the countrymen of Luther, of Goethe, is a portent. Luther was not a Prussian, Goethe was not a Prussian. The heart of the reformer for whom justification was in faith, the heart of the noblest humanist of the latter age—if a throb still stir those hearts, it is of revulsion that their Germany should be under the heel of the Junker.

Shakespeare's ideal state is, as I have tried to show, a state where freemen render service, each in his due degree, and each protected in his service by common interest and right. "Every subject's duty is the king's; but every subject's soul is his own." Shakespeare's state, in its relation with other states, is bounded by legal sanction and regulated by Justice. His great contemporary, the philosopher of that patriotic movement from which America derived its ideals of individual and national liberty and of fraternity with mankind, was of like opinion. Of the Law of Nations, Richard Hooker had written, "There is no reason that any one commonwealth of itself should to the prejudice of another annihilate that whereupon the whole world hath agreed." Precisely of such a state, not a commonwealth but a military despotism and a menace to mankind, annihilating that whereupon the world hath agreed, it is, that Shakespeare prophesied:

> Then everything includes itself in power,
> Power into will, will into appetite,
> And appetite an universal wolf,
> So doubly seconded with will and power,
> Must make perforce an universal prey,
> And last eat up himself.

From the ten thousand British men and women who came to New England between 1620 and 1640, some fifteen million Americans today are descended. From the forty thousand Britons who between 1607 and 1670 settled in Virginia, and from their brothers who colonized the South, some thirty million Americans are descended. From the other Britons who made America their home before and after 1776, perhaps fifteen millions more. All in all, from fifty-five to sixty millions of our one hundred million are exclusively or predominantly British in blood. To these must be added the descendants of the Dutch, the Swedes, the Germans, who in the seventeenth century, and in the eighteenth before 1764, accepting British rule and law and speech, became one folk with the Britons in America and enriched the American spirit with strains of liberality and toleration. Of these, thousands, like Herkimer and Mühlenberg in the War of Independence, stood side by side with Washington.

Since then, and down to 1870, those, and other Europeans who have found a refuge here from the duresse of poverty, social or legal oppression, religious, political, or military tyranny, have gloried in identifying themselves with the inheritors of Anglo-Saxon blood and speech, common law, individual freedom and national responsibility. If it be true that, during the past generation, we have with too light scrutiny admitted to our large freedom and easy fatness tens of thousands whose hands grasp our privileges, but whose hearts still cherish the superstitions of the political inhumanity from which we thought they had escaped, who is to blame? If it be true that we have admitted tens of thousands who, crazed with license, leap to the torch and bomb and in the name of liberty flaunt the rag of anarchy, who is to blame? If we have admitted one hundred thousand ignorant of what America means, and if we acquiesce in that ignorance, who is to blame? Have we too faintly realized our obligation to instruct them in the history, the principles, and the duty of our large freedom, the blame is ours. The time has come for searching of the heart, for open speech; for patient leading toward the light; for exercise of American discipline; for maintenance of American prerogative and dignity. The day of reckoning is upon us: conscious of shortcomings and with humility we face it—but without fear. Not only the Anglo-Saxon majority of the American people but the whole people, in one historic and moral consciousness and one national ideal of democracy finding its soul, goes forth to try that soul, to purge it, to make it real for humanity. Our American heritage is of the revolutionary fathers, of the colonial fathers, of the English founders of colonial liberty—the contemporaries and friends of the poet and prophet of the race. A nation of such inheritance and such hope, can it for a moment tolerate influence or policy or aim subversive of the humanity cherished by the race for ages immemorial? We of the blood, custom, law,—

> We must be free or die, who speak the tongue
> That Shakespeare spake.

APPENDIX

A. Significant Letters, Pamphlets, and Other Data, Relative to the Expedition of 1609.

1. "A Letter of M. Gabriel Archer, touching the Voyage of the Fleet of Ships, which arrived at Virginia, without Sir Tho. Gates, and Sir George Summers, 1609." Archer was recorder of the first colony in Virginia. The letter, apparently to the council at home, is of Aug. 31, 1609, and reached England late in October. It conveyed the first tidings of the tempest of June 24. It speaks of the "contentions, factions, and partakings" in the colony due to the non-arrival of Gates. Printed in 1625 in Purchas his Pilgrimes (Ed. 1906, XIX, 1-4). See also Brown, Genesis, I, 327-332.

2. Vessels begin to return from Virginia late in November, 1609. Sir Thomas Gates and the Sea-Venture supposed lost. Genesis, I, 332-333.

3. Letter of John Radclyffe "To the Right Ho^ble Earle of Salisburye, Lord high Treasurer of England." Dated from Jamestowne, this 4th of October, 1609. Gates and Summers not yet heard of. Captain John Smith reigning as sole governor; but "This man is sent home to answere some misdemeanors." George Percy, president; lack of victuals. Letter arrived late in November, 1609. Not published at the time. In State Papers (Colonial) James I, Vol. I, no. XIX, Genesis, I, 335-335, and Proceedings of the American Antiquarian Society, Worcester, October, 1870, the Letter is given in full.

4. "A True and Sincere Declaration of the Purpose and Ends of the Plantation begun in Virginia." See p. 45, *ante.* By the authority of the Council. S. R. Dec. 14, 1609. Published immediately, as of 1610. The "terrible tempest"; Gates and his company still missing.

5. "A Publication of the Counsell of Virginea, touching the Plantation there." Broadside, printed 1610. See p. 46, *ante.* Published about the same time as no. 4. Reprinted, Genesis, I, 354-356.

6. A Sermon of W. Crashaw, preached in London before Lord De la Warr, Feb. 21, 1610, at his leave-taking for Virginia as Lord Governor. Published with approval of the council, March 19, 1610, under the title "A New-yeeres Gift to Virginea." For extracts see Genesis, I, 360-375.

7. De la Warr sails for Virginia, April 1, 1610. Gates, etc., not yet heard of. Genesis, I, 388.

8. Gates, Somers, and their shipwrecked company sail from Bermuda, May 10, and reach Jamestown, May 23, 1610. Gates finds all things "full of misery and misgovernment," and assumes control, George Percy giving up his commission. See no. 11, below.

9. De la Warr arrives, June 6, just as Gates is abandoning the colony. De la Warr takes over the governorship and, June 12, appoints of his council, Gates, Somers, Percy, Wenman, Newport, William Strachey (secretary and recorder). See no. 11, below.

10. July 15, 1610, Gates and Newport sail for England (see no. 11, below), bearing the following letters (nos. 11, 12, 13). Silvester Jourdan, who wrote no. 14, undoubtedly returned in the same vessel.

11. William Strachey's Letter from Jamestown to an "Excellent Lady" in England, beginning with events of

June 2, 1609, ending July 15, 1610, and sent that day with Gates to England. Not published till 1625, and then as "A True Reportory," etc. See pp. 49–53, *ante.*

12. A letter from Lord De la Warr to the Earl of Salisbury. "Sir Thomas Gates, the bearer thereof." Events of De la Warr's voyage and his arrival in Virginia. "James Towne . . . a verie noysome and unholsome place occasioned much bie the mortalitie and Idlenes of our owne people." Gates is "best able to Informe." The letter is indorsed by Salisbury's secretary—"Received in September, 1610." Printed for first time, State Papers (Colonial) James I, vol. I, no. xxii; also in Genesis, I, 413–415.

13. From the Lord De la Warr to the Patentees in England. This despatch, known also as "Letter of the Governor and Council of Virginia to the Virginia Company of London," is dated July 7, 1610. It is drawn up by Strachey as secretary and includes portions of no. 11, above. Sent with Gates. Not published till 1849 (Hakluyt Society). Also in Genesis, I, 402–413. See pp. 51–52, *ante.*

14. Silvester Jourdan's "A Discovery of the Barmudas." Author's dedication to Master John Fitz James, Esquire, is dated October 13, 1610. Printed by John Windet, London, 1610. Reprinted in 1613 in "A plaine Description of the Barmudas." See no. 10, above, and pp. 45, 48, *ante;* also Genesis, I, 419; II, 620–621.

15. "A True Declaration of the Estate of the Colony of Virginia, etc." S. R. Nov. 8, 1610. Published by order of the council, London: 1610. Based upon Strachey's Letter (no. 11, above) and Gates' Report upon Oath to the Council. See pp. 46, 48–53, *ante.*

16. "Newes from Virginia." A ballad of the voyage,

the shipwreck, the Bermudas, the arrival in Virginia and the return of Gates to England. By R. Rich, Gent, one of the voyage. Published, London: 1610, sold by John Wright. See Genesis, I, 420–426, for copy. Also, probably by the same versifier, since he promises "the same worke more at large," "A ballad called the last News from Virginia," entered at Stationers' Hall by the same bookseller, Aug. 16, 1611. I know of no copy extant.

17. A letter of De la Warr to Salisbury, after his return to England in 1611. Dated June 22. Printed in State Papers (Domestic), and in Genesis, I, 476–477. Also "A short Relation made by the Right Honourable the Lord De la Warr" to the Council, June 25, 1611, "touching his unexpected returne home." Published by authority of the Council (S. R. July 6), 1611. Purchas, XIX, 85–90; Genesis, I, 477–483.

As stated in the body of this volume, the only manuscripts and pamphlets in the foregoing list that could have been of service to Shakespeare in the composition of The Tempest are 4, 11, 14, and 15. Later manuscripts up to February, 1613, such as the letters of Dale to the Council, May 25, 1611, and to Salisbury, Aug. 17, 1611 (the latter with all Strachey's earmarks), Spelman's "Relation" of events from 1609 to 1611, Strachey's "Historie of Travaile into Virginia" of 1612, Whitaker's "Good News from Virginia" of 1612 (published about March, 1613) contain nothing to our purpose. Nor do works printed between 1611 and February, 1613: for instance, "For the Colony in Virginea Britannia, Lawes Divine, Morall and Martiall," 1612; "The New Life of Virginea," 1612; and the two "Oxford Tracts" justifying Captain John Smith's career in the colony, published at Oxford in 1612. Of these, one is "A Map of Virginia with a description of the Country, etc. . . . written by Captaine Smith"; the other, "The Proceedings of the English Colonie in Virginia since their first beginning . . . 1606 till this present 1612, etc.," from the writings of observers in Virginia. "By W. S." W. S. is not, as averred by Malone (Shakespeare, XV, 390) and by Major (Introduction to Strachey's Travaile into Virginia, p. viii), "W. Strachey." Others following the false clue, as for instance Furness, The Tempest (Variorum, IX, 313) are tempted to identify "The Proceedings" by "W. S," printed 1612, with Strachey's True Reportory; and hence the misleading tradition that the True Reportory was published in 1612. The "W. S." above was the Rev. Dr. William Symonds who delivered the sermon "Virginea Britannia" before the company of adventurers and planters, at Whitechapel, April 25, 1609. He was a constant advocate of John Smith. See Eggleston, The Beginners of a Nation, p. 66, and Brown, Genesis, II, 597–601.

B. The True Declaration; the Despatch; the True Reportory.

If the reader will turn to the selections from the latter part of the True Declaration given by Purchas at the end of Strachey's "Letter," or True Reportory, XIX, 67–72, he will notice that the passage from the Declaration, 68, "rather than they would go a stone's cast to fetch wood" agrees with Strachey's De la Warr "Despatch" (Hakluyt Society, Hist. Travaile into Virginia, 1849, p. xxvi) and that the passage, from the Declaration, 67, about "the ground of all those miseries" and "every man would be a Commander" is paralleled in the "Despatch," xxxii–xxxiv, but not verbally. On the other hand the former passage (Declaration, 68) is drawn verbally from Strach-

ey's True Reportory, 45; and the Declaration passage,
from "the ground of all those miseries" to "the fruites of
too deare-bought repentance," is based upon the Reportory, 46–48, 60. The passage in the Declaration, 68–70,
about the treasons, the covetousness in the mariners, the
trucking for corn with the Indians, down to "would not
now obtaine so much as a pottle" is drawn, in spots verbally, from the True Reportory, 50–51. The information
about the "Sturgion" is based upon Reportory, 52. In
the True Declaration, a little further on, the "brackish
water of James fort" is mentioned. This is based upon
Reportory, 58. The accompanying comparison between
"the fennes and marshes" of Jamestown and the Wilds
of Kent is drawn almost verbatim from Reportory, 58–59.
Numerous other sentences and phrases of the Declaration
come from the Reportory.

The first part of the True Declaration is most readily
accessible in Malone, Variorum Shakespeare, XV, or in
Furness, Variorum, IX. If the reader will compare that
with the corresponding sections of the Reportory dealing
with the storm and the description of the Bermudas, he
will find some fifteen precise coincidences of detail or of
speech not duplicated in Jourdan's Discovery. From the
Discovery, this part of the Declaration draws, however,
or appears to draw, five phrases that have no exact parallel
in the Reportory. These are "Summers descryed land";
"the ship fell betwixt two rockes, that caused her to stand
firme"; "an inchaunted pile of rockes"; "unspoyled victuals and tackling"; "to sustaine nature." The Reportory and the Discovery, as I have said in the text,
agree in the report of some salient facts, but they have no
community of literary style. The Despatch has nothing
about the storm.

C. The Excellent Lady.

The Lady to whom Strachey's letter is addressed was vitally concerned in the prosperity of the plantation. Her husband is nowhere mentioned; but among the patentees of 1609 there were no women in their own right, and the informations imparted to this woman are more than once of a kind that could be imparted only to one in close touch with the Virginia Council. She was evidently the wife of one of the more important patentees of 1609; not, however, of one of the eight earls who head the list, for she is nowhere styled "most noble." She is entitled "your Ladiship," "Noble" and, twice, "right Noble Ladie"—of which the last, if it is not merely an epithet, would, according to Elizabethan and Jacobean custom, indicate rank below that of Countess. Of the thirteen succeeding peers in the list of 1609 ten are members of the council. Of the ten, or for that matter all thirteen, the most likely to satisfy the stipulations is Theophilus (since 1603, Baron) Howard of Walden, eldest son of Thomas Howard, Earl of Suffolk. Both father and son were substantial investors in the Company and members of the Council in 1609. The wife of Lord Howard of Walden was Elizabeth, daughter of George Hume, Earl of Dunbar. Their country seat was near the village of Saffron Walden in Essex, which, according to the best authority, appears to have been the home of Strachey himself. The easy, conversational, and sometimes personal tone of Strachey's letter indicates familiar acquaintance with his correspondent. On only one occasion does he specify the previous habitat of any person connected with the voyage or with Virginia, and that is when he tells her ladyship, as a matter of interest to both of them, that one of the Bermuda mutineers, John Want, was "an Essex man of Newport by Saffronwalden."

It may be worth recalling that Hakluyt, who obtained possession of the letter to the Excellent Lady, was long associated with the Howards, as a protégé of the house. In 1598 he had dedicated the second edition of his Navigations to one of the kin, Charles Howard, Earl of Nottingham; and he was, from 1605 on, rector of Wetheringset in Suffolk, not far from Saffron Walden.

D. Bacon and the Liberal Movement.

Bacon became member of the Council for the Virginia Company in 1609. The charters of that year and of 1612, drafted by Sandys, were prepared for the king's signature by Sir Henry Hobart and Sir Francis Bacon. To Bacon's interest in the colony testimony is borne by William Strachey in the Dedication (1618) of a manuscript copy of his Historie of Travaile into Virginia Britannia:[1] "Your Lordship ever approving yourself a most noble fautor [favorer] of the Virginia Plantation, being from the beginning (with other lords and earles) of the principal counsell applyed to propagate and guide yt." In his speech of January 30, 1621, in the House of Commons on the benefits of the king's government occurs the famous passage, "This kingdom now first in his Majesty's Times hath gotten a lot or portion in the New World by the plantation of Virginia and the Summer Islands. And certainly it is with the kingdoms on earth as it is in the kingdom of heaven; sometimes a grain of mustard-seed proves a great tree." A figure already used in the conclusion of the Declaration of the Virginia Council of 1609. In Bacon's essay Of Plantations, completed probably

[1] Sloane MS., No. 1622. An earlier copy dedicated to Sir Allen Apsley, between 1612 and 1616, in Ashmolean MS., No. 1754.

after 1622, and not published till after his death, there appears to be unanimity of practical policy with that of the Sandys party in the council: the shamefulness of planting with "the scum of the people"; the need of centralized but not arbitrary government; the sinfulness of forsaking "a plantation once in forwardness." When it suited his political purpose or when some shadow of liberal concession was harmless, Bacon may have collaborated with Sandys; but his interest in the colony was romantic and always for the glorification of the Crown. "He had no insight into the strength and value of the newer currents that were bearing his countrymen in the direction of a wider and more assured liberty." In some of his Essays he professes to regard the state as an organic unity of king and parliament. But in others he is an outspoken absolutist: the state is sovereign in both religion and politics; those who would subvert the government or depose a king "must be damned and sent to hell forever." Of self-government or of education toward it he has not the faintest glimmer. In his communications intended for the sovereign he is not only absolutist but fulsome to nauseation: Elizabeth has power to enlarge or restrain; James is appointed and gifted of God, his prerogative is unlimited. Bacon was incapable of projecting democratic government at home, still more in a colony beyond the seas.[1] It is inconceivable that friendship or unofficial intercourse of any kind should have existed between Bacon and any of the patriots of the council, such as Southampton, who had followed the Earl of Essex to his death; or between him and any friend of Southampton, like Shakespeare. For it was Bacon who, with an ingratitude

[1] See Gooch, Political Thought from Bacon to Halifax, 22-34.

rarely paralleled, a perfidy to all the instincts of friendship, and a superfluous malignity—in an advocate doubly unjustifiable, had in 1601 "exerted his professional talents to blacken the memory" of his own and Southampton's friend, the Earl of Essex. And by this perfidy he had ensured the conviction of Southampton himself. Though a giant among scientific philosophers, Bacon was in political vision reactionary, and in practice both self-seeking and blind. He had nothing of Hooker's liberalism or Shakespeare's humanity. "He pushed James I towards a collision that could only end in disaster."

E. Indebtedness to Homer, Boethius, Chaucer.

For the heroic strand of his Troilus and Cressida Shakespeare had recourse to Caxton's account of the siege of Troy, and to Homer. The speech of Ulysses is suggested by the second book of the Iliad. Precisely which of the accessible translations, Latin, French or English, Shakepeare was using here—for it is unlikely that he went to the Greek—or what narrative or dramatic manipulation of the story, we do not know. Chapman, whose translation of Books 1, 2, 7–11 had been published in 1598, could not have furnished Shakespeare with the knowledge displayed in the drama of other books of the Iliad than these seven.[1] But in Chapman's second book we find what may have been the verbal origin of Shakespeare's "The specialty of rule hath been neglected"; and "the unworthiest shows as fairly in the mask." Chapman's Ulysses chiding a noisy, discontented Greek, says (Iliad, II, 169–172)—

[1] See J. S. P. Tatlock, The Siege of Troy in Elizabethan Literature, etc. Publ. Mod. Lang. Ass'n of America, XXX, 4, 739 *et seq.*

> Stay, wretch, be still,
And hear thy betters; thou art base, and both in power
  and skill
Poor and unworthy, without name in council or in war.
We must not all be kings. *The rule is most irregular,*
Where many rule. One lord, one king, propose to thee;
  and he,
To whom wise Saturn's son hath given both law and em-
  pery
  To rule the public, is that king.

And from Chapman's translation, a hundred lines before,
of the figure of the bees flocking to their leaders, Shakespeare may have derived something:

> As when of frequent bees
Swarms rise out of a hollow rock, repairing the degrees
Of their egression endlessly, with ever rising new. . .
They still crowd out so; this flock here, that there, be-
  labouring
The loaded flowers; so from their ships and tents the
  army's store
Trooped to these princes and the court.—

From this Shakespeare may have derived something of
both language and figure in the continuation of his Ulysses' speech. For instance, the "Grecian *tents hollow* upon
this plain"; the general "like the *hive* to whom the foragers *repair*"; even the suggestion of his argument concerning "degree,"—though Ulysses uses the word with
a broader significance than Chapman, who himself is
elaborating Homer's simple "tribes of thronging bees
issuing always anew."

Whether through Chapman or not, the first six lines

of Shakespeare's exposition of the specialty of rule (Troilus
and Cressida, I, iii, 78–83), including the simile of the
bees, derive not from Plato or the Platonic tradition, as
some have thought, but from the Iliad.

If Shakespeare was using Chapman's translation of the
Iliad he must have read, a few lines after the passage
about "irregular rule," the words (Il. II, 216–219) with
which Ulysses in the council of the princes prefaces his
cudgeling of Thersites:

Not a worse of all this host came with our king than thee
To Troy's great siege; then do not take into that mouth
    of thine
The names of kings, *much less revile the dignities that shine*
In their supreme states.

Is it too much to imagine that the words italicized above
recalled to Shakespeare's mind the ancient analogy—familiarized by mediæval and renaissance philosophy—of the
celestial dignities performing their motions in wonted order
and degree and held in harmony by the bond of love?

For the love-strand of his play the dramatist is using
Chaucer's Troilus and Criseyde: he has had it by his side
while writing the two preceding scenes of this first act.
He is about to write of the universe held together by the
specialty of rule and of the wreck that ensues when rule
is disregarded. He turns first to Troilus's panegyric of
love (Bk. III, stanzas 250–252), and reads—

    Love, that of erthe and see hath governaunce,
    Love, that *his hestes hath in hevene hye,*
    Love, that with *an holsom alliaunce*
    Halt peples joyned, as him lest them gye . . .

That that the world with feyth, which that is stable,
Dyverseth so his stoundes concordynge,
That elements that been so discordable
Holden a bond perpetuely duringe,
That Phebus mote his rosy day forth bringe,
And that the mone hath lordship over the nightes,
Al this doth Love; ay heried be his mightes!

That that *the see*, that gredy is to flowen,
Constreyneth to a certeyn ende so
His flodes, that so fersly they ne growen
To drenchen erthe and al for ever-mo;
And if that Love ought lete his brydel go,
Al that now loveth a-sonder sholde lepe,
And lost were al, that Love halt now to-hepe.

From this passage Shakespeare turns probably to the original which Chaucer is here versifying, Chaucer's own translation of Boethius De Consolatione Philosophie— it is in the folio before him, Thynne's of 1532 or Speght's of 1598,—and he finds (Bk. II, Metre VIII) one or two other thoughts and expressions that catch his fancy: "so that it is nat leveful [for the see] to strecche hise brode termes or *boundes* up-on the erthes, that is to seyn, to covere al the erthe; al this acordaunce of thinges is *bounden* with Love, *that . . . hath also commaundements to the hevenes.* And yif this Love slakede the brydeles, *alle* thinges that now loven hem to-gederes *wolden maken a bataile continuely. . . .* This Love halt to-gideres poeples joigned with an holy bond, and *knitteth sacrement of mariages* of chaste loves." Or again, in the Boethius (Bk. IV, metre VI), he may note "If thou wilt demen . . . the rightes or the lawes of the heye thonderer, that is to seyn,

of god . . . bihold the heightes of the soverein hevene.
There kepen the sterres by rightful alliaunce of thinges,
hir olde pees . . . And thus maketh Love entrechaunge-
able the perdurable courses; and thus is discordable
bataile y-put out of the contree of the sterres"; or the
phraseology "*Amonges thise thinges sitteth the heye maker,
king* and lord, welle and beginninge, *lawe and wys juge, to
don equitee.*"

Though the controlling power in both these passages is
love, that love is, as with Shakespeare's Ulysses, law. And
if it were not ineffably prosaic to attribute Shakespeare's
thoughts, phrases, figures, precisely to one or another of
many springs of contemporary information and parlance,
in these two passages combined one might say we find the
definite source of some: Sol, enthroned "amids the other";
"like the commandment of a king"; "the unity and married calm of states"; "each thing meets in mere oppugnancy"; "the bounded waters" rising "higher than the
shores" to "make a sop of all this solid globe"; the dis-
ruption of natural loves—"the rude son should strike
his father dead"; "between whose endless jar justice resides."

F. Batman and Rabelais.

In Batman's Additions to Bartholeme (1582) the poet
might have found—if finding of commonplaces were necessary—Sol as a planet, "the fourth in place, as it were a
king in the middest of his throne," and "the Sunne is the
Eye of the world." See New Shakesp. Soc. Trans., 1877–
79, 436–443. And in the French of Rabelais' Gargantua
and Pantagruel or one of the Elizabethan translations of it,
he might have read, perhaps had read, Panurge's famous
panegyric of debtors and borrowers—a correlation backed

by the analogy of planetary interborrowing without which "amongst the planets will be no regular course, all will be disorder." See Urquhart and Motteux, Works of Rabelais, Bk. III, iii, 334–335. But neither Batman nor Rabelais furnished Shakespeare with his materials or his line of thought in this portion of the discourse of Ulysses.

G. Sir Thomas Elyot's The Governour.

In Book I, Chapters one and two, Elyot inveighs against the disorders of a "communaltie," insists upon monarchical government, and elaborates the doctrine of rule by magistrates in their degrees as appointed by the prince. He exemplifies his contention somewhat in the fashion of Ulysses: If the commons "ones throwe downe theyr governour, they ordre every thynge *without justice, only with vengeance and crueltie* . . . Wherefore undoubtedly the best and most sure governaunce is by one kynge or prince. . . . Who can denie but that all thynge in heven and erthe is governed by one god, by one perpetuall ordre, by one providence? One Sunne ruleth over the day, and one Moone over the nyghte; and to descende downe to the erthe, in a littel beest, whiche of all other is moste to be marvayled at, I meane the Bee, is lefte to man by nature, as it semeth, a perpetuall figure of a juste governaunce or rule." From "the discrepance of degrees," he says, "procedeth ordre: whiche in thinges as wel naturall as supernaturall hath ever had such a preëminence, that therby the incomparable majestie of god, as it were by a bright leme of a torche or candel, is declared to the blynde inhabitantes of this worlde. More over *take away ordre from all thynges what shulde than remayne?* Certes nothynge finally, except some man wolde imagine eftsones *chaos;* whiche of some is expounde a *confuse mixture.* Also where

there is any lacke of ordre nedes must be perpetuall con-
flicte." When any agent subject to Nature destroys
order "*he hymselfe of necessite muste than perisshe, whereof
ensuethe universall dissolution.*" And, speaking of order in
the vegetable and animal creation: "without ordre may be
nothing stable or permanent; and it may not be called
ordre, except it do contayne in it *degrees, high and base,*
accordynge to the merite or estimation of the thynge
that is ordered." See Everyman edition, in sequence as
quoted, pages 8–9, 3, 4.

The resemblance in thought, illustration, and occasion-
ally in phraseology, in the passages italicized to the discourse of Ulysses needs no comment. It does not, however,
follow that Shakespeare was deliberately versifying these
half-dozen pages of Elyot. That he may have read the
chapters, steeped his mind in them, is not impossible.
We note, however, that the figure of the celestial order is
but touched upon by Elyot, and the "chaos" but slightly
developed. The indebtedness to Elyot, if any, would begin
and end with the political application of the analogy.

H. Hooker's Indebtedness to Boethius and Arnobius.

"The ordinance which moveth the heaven and the
stars, etc.," is Chaucer's translation of Boethius, De Consolatione, Bk. IV, Metre VI. In the Ecclesiastical Polity,
Bk. I, ii, 6, Hooker quotes Boethius, Bk. IV, Prose V, 50,
*Tamen quoniam bonus mundum rector temperat, recte
fieri cuncta ne dubites,* and translates "Let no man doubt
but that everything is well done, because the world is
ruled by so good a guide." Chaucer's translation of this
runs—"For as moche as god, the good governour, atem-
preth and governeth the world, ne doute thee nat that alle
thinges ben doon a-right."

The reader will find the Latin passage from Arnobius Adversus Gentes in all editions of Hooker's Polity: in the Everyman edition at the bottom of page 157. From it Hooker draws his phraseology: "those principal and mother elements . . . whereof all things are made should lose the qualities which now they have"; "the heavenly arch erected over our heads should loosen and dissolve itself"; "by irregular volubility"; "prince of the lights of heaven." From Arnobius he paraphrases his "moon should wander from her beaten way," his "seasons blend themselves by disordered and confused mixture," his "celestial spheres should forget their wonted motions," his "winds breathe out their last gasp, the clouds yield no rain, the earth be defeated of heavenly influence, the fruits of the earth pine away."

I. Translations and Expositions of Plato and Aristotle Accessible in 1600.

In Plato's Republic, Book IV, 431-2, the comparison of diapason is used. In Book VIII, 562, 574-5, and IX, 574, of the Republic we find something like a suggestion of "strength should be lord of imbecility, and the rude son should strike his father dead"; in VIII, 561, and II, 359, of the three lines beginning "Force should be right"; in VIII, 561 and 564 of lines 119-126—even of the "universal wolf" and of the following passage about "neglection of degree." [1] The Republic was accessible in Latin for eighty-two years before 1600, and in 1600 in the French version of Loys Leroy. Plato's opinion of democracy had, however, for a long time previous been familiar to Englishmen through the fragments of Cicero's De Repub-

[1] J. H. Hanford, A Platonic Passage in Troilus and Cressida; Univ. North Carolina, Studies in Philology, XIII, 2.

lica quoted by St. Augustine in his De Civitate Dei, and to a slight extent through Boethius. Through the Aristotelian tradition and the neo-Platonism of the Renaissance, the Latin and French translations of Aristotle's Politics, and J. D.'s English translation of Leroy's French in 1598, the dangers of democracy had become a political platitude. The expositions of Aristotle and Plato which J. D. had appended to his translation would have familiarized those who read nothing but English with the opinions in general of both philosophers. The psychology developed in Plato's Republic had lived through his Timæus during the thousand years in which the Republic seemed to sleep; and, in Aristotelian guise, it had dominated the schools during the middle ages. Of the Nicomachean Ethics of Aristotle there existed numerous translations in Shakespeare's day, an English paraphrase by Wylkinson, of 1547, and a French translation by de Plessis, of 1553. For reasons given in the text I do not believe that Shakespeare was deriving the politics, psychology or ethics of Ulysses' speech directly from either Plato or Aristotle.

J. The Ethics and Psychology of Hooker and Shakespeare.

1. Shakespeare's dicta concerning the nature and apprehension of right and wrong, absolute and relative values, and the whole question of choice, closely resemble at times the utterances of Montaigne, but the substantial philosophy, that which inspires his rule of conduct, is more explicitly and logically expounded by Hooker. The reflections of the Friar in Romeo and Juliet, II, iii, 17 (*c.* 1594–6) on the special good that may proceed from vileness, and *vice versa;* Henry V's "There is some soul of goodness in things evil, would men observingly distil it out," IV, 1, 4

(1599)—both written before Florio's translation of Montaigne was published; Hamlet's "There is nothing either good or bad, but thinking makes it so," II, ii, 256 (1602–4); the query of Troilus (1602–9), "What is aught but as 'tis valued?" Hector's reply (II, ii, 53–57):

> But value dwells not in particular will;
> It holds his estimate and dignity
> As well wherein 'tis precious of itself
> As in the prizer: 'tis mad idolatry
> To make the service greater than the god;

and Troilus's retort (61–67):

> I take to-day a wife, and my election
> Is led on in the conduct of my will,
> My will enkindled by mine eyes and ears,
> Two traded pilots twixt the dangerous shores
> Of will and judgment: how may I avoid,
> Although my will distaste what is elected,
> The wife I chose;—

all these find their counterpart, if counterpart must be found for reflections which might be common to the thought of the age, in the four or five sections of Hooker's Polity (I, vii–xi), some thirty pages in all. For instance, "To choose is to will one thing before another. And to will is to bend our souls to the having or doing of that which they see to be good. Goodness is seen with the eye of the understanding"; and in what follows—"there is no particular object so good but it may have the show of unpleasant quality," wherefore "the will may shrink and decline it; there is no particular evil which hath not some appearance of goodness whereby to insinuate itself. For evil as evil cannot be desired: if that be desired which is evil, the cause is the goodness which is or seemeth to be joined with it. Goodness doth not move by being, but by being apparent; and therefore many things are neglected which are most precious, only because the value of them lieth hid . . . All particular things which are subject unto action the Will doth so far forth incline unto, as Reason judgeth them the better for us. . . . If Reason err we fall into evil. . . . The greatest part of men are such as prefer their private good before all things, even that good which is sensual before whatsoever is most divine. . . . Unless the last good of all, which is desired altogether for itself, be also infinite, we do evil in making it our end. . . . Whereas we now love the thing that is good especially in respect of benefit unto us; we shall then love the thing that is good, only or principally for the goodness of beauty in itself." [1]

"The web of our life is of a mingled yarn," says one in All's Well that Ends Well (as we have it, probably of 1602), "good and ill together; our virtues would be proud if our faults whipped them not; and our crimes would despair if they were not cherished by our virtues." "Of such perfection capable we are not in this life," says Hooker. "While we are in the world, subject we are unto sundry imperfections, griefs of body, defects of mind; yea, the best things we do are painful, and the exercise of them grievous;" but again—"We are not to marvel at the choice of evil then when the contrary is probably known. . . . For there was never sin committed, wherein a less good was not preferred before a greater, and that wilfully." [2]

[1] Polity, 169–170, 172, 174, 192, 202, 205.
[2] Polity, 203, 173.

2. The Law of Nature and of Political Society. "Nature craves," says Hector (Troilus and Cressida, II, ii, 173–182),

> Nature craves
> All dues be render'd to their owners: now,
> What nearer debt in all humanity
> Than wife is to the husband? If this law
> Of nature be corrupted through affection,
> And that great minds, of partial indulgence
> To their benumbed wills, resist the same,
> There is a law in each well-order'd nation
> To curb those raging appetites that are
> Most disobedient and refractory.

The thought is not rare. It occurs also in Hooker (I, x, 1)—"We see then how nature itself teacheth laws and statutes to live by. . . . Laws politic, ordained for external order and regiment among men, are never framed as they should be, unless presuming the will of man to be inwardly obstinate, rebellious, and averse from all obedience unto the sacred laws of his nature, . . . they do accordingly provide notwithstanding so to frame his outward actions, that they be no hinderance unto the common good for which societies are instituted; unless they do this, they are not perfect. . . . Laws do not only teach what is good, but they enjoin it, they have in them a certain constraining force." [1]

3. The principle that nought is ours save as we use it comes to the fore in Ulysses' colloquy with Achilles (Troilus and Cressida, III, iii, 95 *et seq.*):

[1] Polity, 187–8, 192.

> A strange fellow here
> Writes me that "Man—how dearly ever parted,
> How much in having, or without or in—
> Cannot make boast to have that which he hath,
> Nor feels not what he owes, but by reflection;
> As when his virtues shining upon others
> Heat them, and they retort that heat again
> To the first giver."

Achilles finds no strangeness here at all and cites the analogy of the soul and the eye that cannot "behold itself, not going from itself"—a commonplace from the pseudo-Platonic First Alcibiades (Latin transl. 1560), by way, perhaps, of Cicero's Tusculans (English transl. 1561) or Davies Nosce Teipsum (1599), or of general conversation. Ulysses, returning to his "strange fellow," replies,

> I do not strain at the position,—
> It is familiar,—but at the author's drift;
> Who, in his circumstance, expressly proves
> That no man is the lord of anything,
> (Though in and of him there be much consisting,)
> Till he communicate his parts to others.

The thought is expressed by other Shakespearian characters. Vincentio has even more poetically phrased it in Measure for Measure of 1603-4 (I, i, 30 *et seq.*): "Thyself and thy belongings are not thine own; . . . Heaven doth with us as we with torches do; . . . Spirits are not finely touched but to fine issues; . . . Nature . . . determines . . . both thanks and use"; and his Laertes (Hamlet, IV, v, 160–162) is yet to rephrase it. That Hooker, also, insists upon the principle is not strange; nor, if Shakespeare had to borrow this thought from the divine, would he be likely to write him down "a strange fellow." "To supply those defects and imperfections," writes Hooker (Eccl. Pol. I, x, 1, and 12), "which are in us living single and solely by ourselves, we are naturally induced to seek communion and fellowship with others. . . . Between men and beasts there is no possibility of sociable communion, because the well-spring of that communion is a natural delight which man hath to transfuse from himself into others, and to receive from others into himself especially those things wherein the excellency of his kind doth most consist. . . . Civil society doth more content the nature of man than any private kind of solitary living, because in society this good of mutual participation is so much larger than otherwise." And, in XI, 1, "All things (God only excepted), besides the nature which they have in themselves, receive externally some perfection from other things, as hath been shewed. Insomuch as there is in the whole world no one thing great or small, but either in respect of knowledge or of use it may add unto our perfection somewhat."[1]

I cite these passages merely as further example of similarity in subject and point of view. Not only is the "position familiar" as Ulysses says, and frequently taken in the plays of Shakespeare and in his sonnets, it abounds also in plays, essays and sonnets of others, Italian, French, English. If Shakespeare derived the "position" from any definite source, it might have been the pseudo-Platonic, as mentioned above, or the Nosce Teipsum, or the discussion of Friendship in the Ethics of Aristotle, or, as J. M. Robertson has shown,[2] one of several passages, in Cicero,

[1] Polity, 188, 198, 201.
[2] Montaigne and Shakespeare, pp. 101 *et seq.*

Seneca, Erasmus, Montaigne, or Marston. Or it may have been from Hooker. For the strange fellow, however, and his "drift"—the circumstantial detail, which Ulysses counts less familiar—I venture to suggest, though I suppose others have done the same, Rabelais, who was well known to the Elizabethans, and his Panurge's panegyric upon Borrowing. See the Works of Rabelais, III, iii, v, pages 333-343, in Motteux's translation. Rabelais was a stranger fellow than Socrates, Aristotle, Montaigne or Hooker. And the drift of Panurge's "circumstance" is stranger still.

4. Discourse of Reason; Will and Appetite. We cannot be sure that Shakespeare used the expression "discourse of reason" before 1604. It occurs in Troilus and Cressida, published first in 1609 with additions, and it may have been in the original manuscript of about 1601-2. It occurs in the 1604 quarto of Hamlet (written about 1601-2), but not in the incomplete version published in 1603. It appears as "discourse of thought" in Othello, written and acted about 1604, but not published till 1622. The expression has been discovered in a few English books published before 1580; but there is no proof that any of them were read by Shakespeare. Bacon uses the phrase in 1599 (putative pamphlet on Squire's conspiracy), and in The Advancement of Learning, 1605.[1] J. M. Roberston finds the expression four times in Montaigne's Essays and in Florio's translation of them, published in 1603. He concedes that the words "seem to be scholastic in origin" but he finds it difficult to "doubt that . . . it came to Shakespeare through Florio's Montaigne." The phrase is scholastic, but it was probably in common use in Eliza-

[1] J. M. Robertson, Montaigne and Shakespeare, p. 47. See also, Furness, Variorum, Hamlet, I, p. 45; and N. E. D.

bethan conversation. I find "discourse," "discourse of reason," "discourse of natural reason," "natural discourse of reason," "natural reason," "natural discourse" scattered up and down the pages of Hooker's Polity, 1594. In the first book Hooker uses the phrase in several of its variations. He discusses the faculty of reason, and regards "discourse" as the art or process of ratiocination. "The Law of Reason or Human Nature," he says (I, x, 8) "is that which men by discourse of natural reason have rightly found out themselves to be all for ever bound unto in their actions." In the third book, speaking of the disparagement of reason by the Puritans, he says (viii, 11) "Let men be taught this [the belief in God's existence, etc.] either by revelation from heaven, or by instruction upon earth. . . . If the knowledge thereof were possible without discourse of natural reason, why should none be found capable thereof but only men?" And on the same page, "What science can be attained unto without the help of natural discourse and reason?" A few paragraphs earlier (VIII, 7) Hooker contrasts genuine philosophy as "true and sound knowledge attained by natural discourse of reason" with "that philosophy which to bolster heresy or error casteth a fraudulent show of reason upon things which are indeed unreasonable." And, in the last paragraph of the same section, "human laws" are defined to be "ordinances, which such as have lawful authority given them for that purpose do probably draw from the law of nature and God, by discourse of reason aided with the influence of divine grace." [1]

To attribute Shakespeare's use of the expression to the exclusive authority of Hooker would be as unwarrantable as to attribute it to a reading of Bacon's pamphlet on

[1] Polity, 182, 319, 312, 324.

Squire's conspiracy, or of his Advancement of Learning[1]
in manuscript, say, of 1603, or of Florio's Montaigne
whether in the print of 1603 or in manuscript before publication, or of any other English books, in which we know
it was used before 1601. It is worth noticing, however,
that, outside of the Polity, in none of these books, even
by Bacon or Montaigne, is the phrase used other than
calamo currente save once, when Montaigne[2] in the Essay
on Spurina vouchsafes, "It is much, by discourse of reason,
to bridle our appetites." As to the word "discourse"
in the sense of drawing inferences, it appears frequently
in Montaigne, but that fact combined with Montaigne's
four incidental mentions of "discourse of reason" does not
justify Mr. Robertson in concluding that Shakespeare
derives word or phrase from Montaigne. Nor does it
follow that Hamlet's soliloquy "What is a man, etc.,"
is an "echo" of Montaigne, Bk. II, 8—"Since it hath
pleased God to endow us with some capacity of discourse,
that as beasts we should not servilely be subjected to
common laws, but rather with judgment and voluntary
liberty apply ourselves unto them; . . . only reason ought
to have the conduct of our inclinations"; and of Bk. II,
18, "Nature hath endowed us with a large faculty to en-
tertain ourselves apart, etc." In Hooker, "discourse"
or discourse of reason"—the argumentative process by
which we determine the value of "things unsensible"—
is clearly discriminated, on the one hand, from judgment
common to us with the beasts, concerning matters of
appetite, and on the other, from processes of supernatural
revelation. By Hooker it is much more largely and explicitly discussed than by Montaigne or any other con-

[1] Bk. I, p. 28, l. 13, W. A. Wright's edition, 1885.
[2] Bk. II, XXXIII, p. 296, Temp. Class Ed.

temporary writer to whom Shakespeare had access. In other words, if without going back to Plato, Aristotle, and works of mediæval philosophy we have to fix upon a printed source for the psychology and ethics underlying Shakespeare's poetry of the "discourse of reason," the argument for Hooker's Polity is more easy to maintain than for any other so far adduced.

In order that we may examine the underlying psychology and ethics let us quote from the poet the passages under consideration. In Troilus and Cressida (II, ii, 115–116), Hector remonstrates with the impetuous Troilus:

> Is your blood
> So madly hot that no discourse of reason,
> Nor fear of bad success in a bad cause,
> Can qualify the same.

In Othello (IV, ii, 152–153) Desdemona protests that her will never did trespass against Othello's love, "Either in discourse of thought or actual deed." In Hamlet of the 1604 quarto the hero (I, ii, 143–151) soliloquizes:

> Must I remember. Why, she would hang on him
> As if increase of appetite had grown
> By what it fed on[1] . . . Why she, even she—
> Oh God! a beast that wants discourse of reason
> Would have mourned longer!—[2]

and again (IV, iv, 33–39):[3]

[1] Q. 1603 has: "looked on" for "fed on."
[2] Q. 1603 has "Oh, God a beast Devoid of reason would not have made such speed."
[3] Not in Q. 1603.

What is a man,
If his chief good and market of his time
Be but to sleep and feed? a beast, no more.
Sure He that made us with such large discourse,
Looking before and after, gave us not
That capability and godlike reason
To fust in us unused. Now whether it be
Bestial oblivion, or some craven scruple
Of thinking too precisely on the event,—
A thought which quarter'd hath but one part wisdom
And ever three parts coward,—I do not know
Why yet I live to say "This thing's to do;"
Sith I have cause and will and strength and means
To do't.

Let us compare with these extracts the thought of
Hooker, noting especially the words which I have italicized,
and remembering that we are already familiar with his
usage of "discourse of reason."   In Bk. I of the Polity,
we read of "that inferior natural desire which we call
Appetite:

"*The object of Appetite is whatsoever sensible good may be
wished for; the object of Will is that good which Reason doth
lead us to seek.* Affections as joy, and grief, and fear, and
anger, with such like, being as it were the sundry fashions
and forms of Appetite, can neither rise at the conceit of a
thing indifferent, *nor yet choose but rise* at the sight of certain things. *Wherefore it is not altogether in our power,
whether we will be stirred with affections or no;* whereas
*actions which issue from the disposition of the Will are in the
power thereof to be performed or stayed,* (170) . . . Sensible
goodness is *most apparent, near and present, which causeth
the Appetite to be therewith strongly provoked* (172) . . .

The rule of natural agents which work after a sort of their own accord, *as the beasts do,* is the judgment of common sense or fancy *concerning the sensible goodness* of those objects wherewith they are moved (177) . . . It may be therefore a question whether those operations of men are to be counted voluntary, *wherein that good which is sensible provoketh Appetite* and Appetite causeth action, *Reason being never called to counsel; as when we eat or drink, and betake ourselves unto rest,* and such like (170) . . . *What things are food and what are not we judge naturally by sense; neither need we any other law* to be our director in that behalf *than the selfsame which is common unto us with beasts* (229) . . . The soul of man being *capable of a more divine perfection* hath . . . a further ability, whereof in them [the beasts] there is no show at all, *the ability of reaching higher than unto sensible things* (167) . . . *By reason* man attaineth unto the knowledge of things that are and are not sensible. . . . Man in perfection of nature being made according to the *likeness of his Maker resembleth him also in the manner of working* (169) . . . . Yea, those men which have no written law of God to show what is good or evil, carry *written in their hearts* the universal law of mankind, *the Law of Reason, whereby they judge as by a rule which God hath given unto all men* for that purpose (228) . . . And the Law of Reason or human nature is that which men *by discourse of natural Reason* have rightly found out themselves *to be all for ever bound unto in their actions* (182) . . . Man doth seek a triple perfection: first, a sensual; . . . then an intellectual consisting in those things *which none underneath man is either capable of* or acquainted with; *lastly, a spiritual and divine, consisting in those things whereunto we tend* by supernatural means here, but cannot here attain unto them" (205).

By virtue of reason we look "before and after"; for as Hooker says: "Goodness is seen with the eye of the understanding. And the light of that eye, is reason (170) . . . And of discerning goodness there are but then two ways; the one the knowledge of the *causes* whereby it is made such; the other the observation of those signs and tokens" from which we argue that where they are, goodness will be found, "though we know not the cause by force whereof it is there" (175). No less fundamental to his discussion is the premise that reason must not, as Hamlet says, "fust in us unused." "Through neglect thereof [of Reason]," Hooker reminds us, "*abused we are with the show of that which is not:* sometimes the subtlety of Satan inveighing us as it did Eve; sometimes the hastiness of our Wills preventing the more considerate advice of sound Reason. . . . The search of knowledge is a thing painful; and *the painfulness of knowledge is that which maketh the Will so hardly inclinable thereunto*" (173); and then, "the soul *preferreth rest in ignorance* before wearisome labor to know" (174). Moreover, "there is no particular object so good, but *it may have the show of some difficulty or unpleasant quality annexed to it, in respect whereof the Will may shrink and decline it*" (172).

There may be nothing in the poetic phrasing or the dramatic passion of the "discourse of reason" passages in Troilus and Cressida and Hamlet, or in the passage of similar psychological and ethical import concerning "power into will, will into appetite" from the former play to establish beyond shadow of doubt that Shakespeare derived the inspiration from Hooker alone; but the verbal similarities are striking, and the philosophical trend of these and other passages is in every particular paralleled by that of the judicious divine. And with but two or three exceptions the parallels fall within the compass of one very small book.

5. It is an established fact that Shakespeare had read Montaigne, and probably in Florio's translation. Everybody knows that he took Gonzalo's description of the commonwealth where there is "no occupation; all men idle, all" from the original Montaigne or the translation, and that more than one other passage comes from one or the other—probably the translation. But the induction from resemblances to the authentic inspiration of a specific writer may be carried to perilous conclusions. For in any generation many thinkers will express themselves in similar fashion. Mr. Robertson[1] finds "a noteworthy resemblance" between "a paragraph in the Apology of Raimond Selonde[2] in which Montaigne sets over against each other the splendour of the universe and the littleness of man," and Hamlet's address to Rosencrantz and Guildenstern (II, ii, 319–321), beginning "This most excellent canopy" and concluding: "What a piece of work is man! how noble in reason! how infinite in faculties! in form and moving how express and admirable! in action how like an angel! in apprehension how like a god! the beauty of the world! the paragon of animals! And yet, to me what is this quintessence of dust?"

Says Mr. Robertson, "Here the thought diverges, Shakespeare making it his own as he always does, and altering its aim; but the language is curiously similar." I find as fruitful similarity between Hamlet's view of man's quality and place in the universe and the view offered by Hooker.

[1] Montaigne and Shakespeare, 52–55.
[2] "Let us see what holdfast" to "equal himself to God." Florio's Montaigne's Essays, Bk. II, 12, pp. 203–208 (Temp. Cl. ed.)

Shakespeare's supremely poetic apostrophe required of course no model. But Hooker, having discussed the eternal law concerning "things natural which are not in the number of voluntary agents"—the celestial spheres, our earth among them, says (Book I, iv)—"Now that we may lift up our eyes (as it were) from the footstool to the throne of God, and leaving these natural, consider a little the state of heavenly and divine creatures; touching Angels, which are spirits unmaterial and intellectual, the glorious inhabitants of those sacred palaces. . . . God which moveth mere natural agents as an efficient only, doth otherwise move intellectual creatures, and especially his holy angels (161). Desire to resemble him in goodness maketh them unweariable . . . to do all manner of good unto all the creatures of God, but especially unto the children of men: in the countenance of whose nature looking downward, they behold themselves beneath themselves; even as upward in God . . . *they see that character which is nowhere but in themselves and us resembled.* . . . *Angelical actions* may be reduced unto these three general kinds: first, most delectable love arising from the *visible apprehension of the purity, glory, and beauty of God,* invisible saving only unto spirits that are pure; secondly, adoration . . . thirdly, imitation (162). . . . Thus much therefore may suffice for angels, the next unto whom in degree are men (164). . . . By proceeding in the knowledge of truth, and by growing in the exercise of virtue, man amongst the creatures of this inferior world aspireth to the greatest conformity with God (165). . . . With Plato what one thing more usual than to excite men unto love of wisdom by showing how much wise men are thereby exalted above men; *how knowledge* doth raise *them up into heaven; how it maketh them though not gods, yet as gods,*

high, *admirable*, and *divine?*. . . From utter vacuity
they grow till they come at length to *be even as the angels
are*" (166).

Hooker, as quoted earlier, next shows that "the soul of
man being capable of a more divine perfection hath (besides the *faculties* of growing unto sensible knowledge
which is common unto us with beasts) *the ability of reaching higher than unto sensible things*" (167), *viz.*, reason; and
that "man *in perfection of nature being made according to
the likeness of his Maker* resembleth him also in the manner
of working. . . . And that which is good in the *actions*
of men [as above in "angelical actions"], doth not only
delight as profitable, but as amiable also. In which consideration the Grecians most divinely have given to the
active perfection of men a name expressing both *beauty*
and goodness. (175). . . . And is it possible that Man
being not only *the noblest creature in the world*, but even a
very world in himself, his transgressing the Law of his
Nature should draw no manner of harm after it? (185).
. . . What he coveteth as good in itself, toward that his
desire is ever *infinite* (202). . . . No good is infinite but
only God; therefore He our felicity and bliss (203). . . .
*Under Man, no creature in the world is capable of felicity
and bliss*" (204).

There are resemblances between Hamlet's "To be or not
to be" soliloquy and passages in Montaigne's twelfth
essay of the Third Book:[1] notably between "take arms
against a sea of troubles" and Montaigne's "Loe here
another huddle or tide of mischiefe, that on the neck of
the former came rushing upon mee"; between Hamlet

[1] Printed in parallel columns by Miss E. R. Hooker, Relation
of Shakespeare to Montaigne (Publ. Mod. Lang. Ass'n Amer.,
N. S., X, 3, 354–355).

on Death—" 'Tis a consummation devoutly to be wished" and Florio's translation of *anéantissement*, etc.—"If it be a consummation of one's being, it is also an amendment and entrance into a long and quiet night"; and of the metaphorical sequence in both: to die; to sleep; to dream or not. For these portions of the soliloquy there are no analogies in Hooker; but if the reader think it worth while to unearth resemblances between Shakespeare's thought and diction and the thought and diction of some writer of contemporary note, let me refer him again to the half-dozen lines of this soliloquy beginning "The oppressor's wrong, the proud man's contumely" and the clause in Hooker's Polity (196) about the punishment of contumely and wrong offered unto any of the common sort" (already quoted, p. 188, *ante*). Perhaps, also, in the conclusion of the soliloquy, where the will is described as puzzled by uncertainty of thought, reason or consciousness—

> Thus conscience doth make cowards of us all;
> And thus the native hue of resolution
> Is sicklied o'er with the pale cast of thought,
> And enterprises of great pith and moment
> With this regard their currents turn awry,
> And lose the name of action—

he may find some reflex of, or similarity to, Hooker's exposition in the Polity (I, vii, 6–viii, 2, pages 172–175): "There is no particular object so good, but it may have the show of some difficulty or unpleasant quality annexed to it, in respect whereof the Will may shrink and decline it. . . . Whereas therefore amongst so many things as are to be done, there are so few, the goodness whereof Reason in such sort doth or easily can discover, we are not to marvel at the choice of evil even then when the contrary is probably known. . . . The painfulness of knowledge is that which maketh the will so hardly inclinable thereunto. . . . By reason of that original weakness in the instruments, without which the understanding part is not able in this world by discourse to work, the very conceit of painfulness is as a bridle to stay us. . . . If Reason err, we fall into evil, and are so far forth deprived of the general perfection we seek. . . . As the straight way is most acceptable to him that travelleth, because by it he cometh soonest to his journey's end; so in action that which doth lie the evenest between us and the end we desire must needs be the fittest for our use. . . . Of discerning goodness, . . . the knowledge of the causes whereby it is made such . . . is the more sure and infallible way, but so hard that all shun it, and had rather walk as men do in the dark by haphazard, than tread so long and intricate mazes for knowledge' sake." There may be in Hamlet's "native hue of resolution . . . sicklied o'er by the pale cast of thought" no adaptation of Hooker's "very conceit of the painfulness" of knowledge, which is "as a bridle to stay" the will from action,—but merely a similarity in the balancing of probabilities about a common problem.

In all that I have said about conjectural sources for expressions that were or may have been proverbial, and for trends of thought that might have occurred to any poet conversant with contemporary science and speculation, my purpose has been not to assert indebtedness, implicit or verbal, but to call attention to coincidences. The cumulative evidence of similarities may persuade some that Shakespeare had read the Ecclesiastical Polity. Whether he had read it or not, it is certain that about many things he thought much as Hooker did, and about many wrote much in the same way.

INDEX

Printed in the United States of America

Printed in the United States
37118LVS00003B/77